Operating System

Dr.E. Ramaraj

Dr.D. Napoleon

Published by

Operating System

ISBN 978-93-85477-59-1

Authors

Dr.E. Ramaraj

Dr.D. Napoleon

Bonfring

309, 2nd Floor, 5th Street Extension, Gandhipuram,

Coimbatore-641 012.

Tamilnadu, India.

E-mail: info@bonfring.org

Website: www.bonfring.org

Phone: 0422 4213231

<table>
<tr><th>Chapter</th><th>Contents</th><th>Page No</th></tr>
</table>

CHAPTER-1

INTRODUCTION

A modern computer system consists of one or more Processors, some main memory, disks, Printers, a keyboard, a display, network interfaces, and other input/output devices. All in all, a complex system, writing programs that keep track of all these components and uses them correctly, by letting alone optimally when operates on an extremely difficult job. For this reason, computers are equipped with a layer of software called the operating system, whose job is to manage all these devices and provide user programs with a simpler interface to the hardware. These systems are the subject of this book.

1.1.   What is an Operating System

Operating System (OS) is a set of system programs which provides an environment to help the user to execute the programs. The OS is a resource manager which allocates and manages various resources like Processor(s), main memory, input/output devices and information (files) on secondary memory devices. The purpose of studying OS concepts is to understand the capabilities and limitations of this resource manager. An understanding of the concepts helps in writing effective programs. Operating Systems is an integrated set of Programs that controls the resources (CPU, Memory, I/O devices etc) of a computer system and provides its users with an interface or virtual machine that is easier to use than the bare machine. According to this definition, the two primary objectives of an operating system are:

1)   Making a computer system easier to user.
2)   Manage the resources of a computer system.

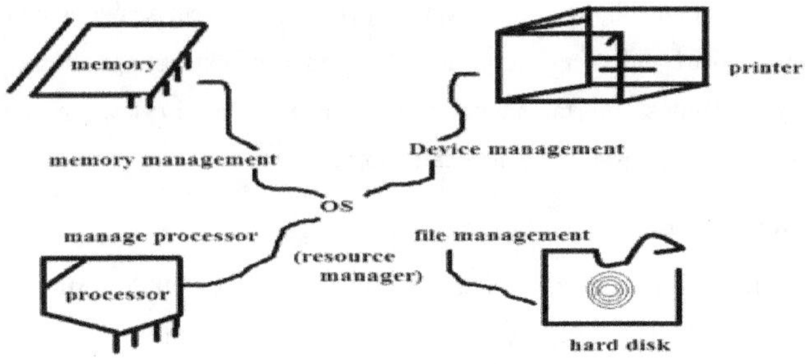

Figure 1: Operating System Service

Make a Computer System Easier to Use

An operating system hides the details of the hardware resources from programmers and other users to provide them with a convenient interface for using computer system. It acts as an intermediary between the hardware and its users, providing a high level interface to low-level hardware resources, and making it easier for programmers and other users to use those resources.

Figure 2: Logical Architecture of a Computer System

Figure 2 shows the logical architecture of a computer system. As shown, hardware resources are surrounded by operating system layer that, in turn, is surrounded by a layer of other System software and a set of application Programs processing applications, scientific and engineering applications, entertainment and educational, end users view the computer system in terms of the user interfaces of the application programs.

Manage the Resources of a Computer System

An operating system manages all the resources of a computer system. This involves performing such tasks as to keeping track of who is using which resource, granting resource requests, accounting for resource usage, and mediating conflicting requests from different programs and users. Efficient and fair sharing of system resources among user and/or Programs is a key goal of all operating systems.

1.1.1. Measuring System Performance

Efficiency of an operating system and overall Performance of a computer system are measured usually in terms of the following parameters:

1) Throughput: Throughput is the amount of work that a system is able to do per unit time. It is measure as the number of Processes completed by the system in per unit time. For example, if a system is able to complete n process in t seconds, its throughput is n/t process per second during that interval. Throughput is measured normally in process/hour. Note that the system does not depend only on its Jobs Processing efficiency, but also on the nature of Jobs processed. For a long process, throughput of a system may be one process/hour; whereas for short processes, it may be 100 processes/hour for the same system.

2) Turnaround time: From the user's point of view of an individual user, an important criterion is how long it takes a system to complete a job submitted by him/her. Turnaround time is the interval between the times of submission of a Job to the system for Processing to the time of completion of the Job. Although, higher throughput is desirable from the point of view of overall system performance, individual users are more interested in better turnaround time for their jobs.

3) Response time: Turnaround time is not a suitable measure for interactive systems because in such a system process can produce some outputs early during its execution and can continue executing while previous results are being output to the user. Hence, another measure used in case of interactive system is response time. It is the interval between the time of submission of a Job to the system for Processing to the time of the system producing the first response for the Job.

In any computer system, it is desirable to maximize throughput and minimize turnaround time and response time.

1.2.   Main Functions of an Operating System

Most operating system perform the functions given below. A separate module of operating system software performs each of these functions.

1) Process Management

Process Management module takes care of creation and deletion of processes, scheduling of system resources to different processes which requests them, and providing mechanisms for synchronization and communication among Processes.

2) *Memory Management*

A memory management module takes care of allocation and de–allocation of memory space to programs which are in need of this resource.

3) *File Management*

File management module takes care of file–related activities such as organization, storage, retrieval naming, sharing and protection of files.

4) *Security*

Security module protects the resource and information of a computer system against destruction and unauthorized access.

5) *Command Interpretation*

Command interpretation module takes care of interpreting user commands, and directing system resources to process the commands. With this mode of interaction with a system users are not much concerned about hardware details of the system.

1.1.2. The Operating System as an Extended Machine

The function of the operating system is to present the user with the equivalent of an extended machine or virtual machine that is easier to program than the underlying hardware. However, the operating system achieve this goal is a long story, which we will study in detail throughout this book. To summarize it in a nutshell the operating system provides a variety of services that programs can obtain using special instructions called system calls.

1.3. History of Operating Systems

1.3.1. First Generation (1945 – 1955)

1) Vacuum Tubes
2) Plug boards

In this generation, all succeeded in building calculating engines. In earlier days mechanical relays were used they were very slow, with cycle time which as measured in seconds. Relays were later replaced by vacuum tubes. These machines were enormous, filling up entire rooms with tens of thousands of vacuum tubes, but they were still millions of times slower than even the cheapest personal computers available today. In those earliest days a single group of people designed, built, programmed, operated and maintained each machine. All programming was done in absolute machine language, by often writing up plug boards to control the machine's basic functions. Programming languages were unknown (even assembly language was unknown).

1.3.2. The Second Generation (1955 – 1965)

1) Transistors

2) Batch system

The introduction of the transistors in the mid of 1950s changed the picture radically. Computers became reliable enough that they could be manufactured and sold to paying customers with the expectation that they could continue to function long enough to get some useful work done for the first time, there was a clear separation between designers, builders, operators, programmers and maintenance personnel. These machines are now called main frame computers.

When the computer finished whatever job it was currently running, an operator would go over to the printer and teen off the output and carry it over to the output room, so that the programmer could collect it later. Then he would take one of the card decks that had been brought from the input room and read it in. If the FORTAN computer was needed, the operator have to get it from the file cabinet and read it in. Much computer time was wasted while operators were walking around the machine room. Given the high cost for the equipment, it is not surprising that people quickly looked for ways to reduce the wasted time. The solution generally adopted was the batch system.

1.3.3. The Third Generation (1965 -1980)

1) ICs

2) Multiprogramming

By the early 1960's most computer manufacturers had two distinct, and totally incompatible, product lines. On the one hand there were the word–oriented, large–scale scientific computers, such as the 7094, which were used for normal numerical calculations in science and engineering. On the other hand, there was the character oriented, commercial computers, such as the 1401, which was widely used by the banks and insurance companies for sorting and printing. Developing and maintaining two completely different product lines was an expensive proposition for the manufactures. In addition, many new computer customer initially needed a small machine but later outgrew it and wanted a bigger machine that would run all their old programs, but faster. IBM attempted to solve both of these problems at a single stroke by introducing the system/360. The 360 was a series of software–compatible machines ranging from 1401–sized which was more powerful than the 7084. The machines differed only in price and performance. Since all the machines had the same architecture and instruction set, programs written for one machine could run on all the others, at least in theory. Furthermore, the 360 was designed to handle both scientific and commercial computing. Thus a single family of machines could satisfy the needs of all customers. In subsequent years, IBM has come out with compatible successors to the 360 line, using more modern technology, known as the 370, 4300, 3080 and 3090 series.

1.3.4.   The Fourth Generation (1980–present)

1)   Personal Computers

With the development of LSI (large scale integration) circuits, chips containing thousands of transistors on a square centimetre of silicon, the age of the personal computer dawned. In terms of architecture, Personal computers (initially called Microcomputers) were not all that different from minicomputers of the PDP- 11 class, but in terms of price they certainly were different. Where the mini computer made it possible for a department in a company or university to have its own computer, the microprocessor chip made it possible for a single individual to have his or her personal computers.

In 1974 when Intel came out with the 8080, the first general – purpose 8 bit CPU, it wanted an operating system for the 8080, in part to be able to list it. In 1977, Digital Research rewrote CP/M to make it suitable for running on the many microcomputers using the 8080, Zilog Z80 and other CPU chips. Many application problems were written to run on CP/M allowing it to completely dominate the world of micro computing for about 5 years.

In the early 1980's IBM designed the IBM PC and looked around for software to run on it. By the time, in 1983 the IBM PC/AT came out with the Intel 80286 CPU, MS- DOS was firmly entrenched and CP/M was on its last legs. MS- DOS was later widely used on the 80386 and 80486. Although the initial version of MS- DOS was family primitive, subsequent versions included more advanced features, including many taken from UNIX.

Linux is an open–source operating system enhanced and backed by thousands of programmers world wide web. It is a multitasking, multiprocessing operating system designed originally the use on personal computer. The name "Linux" is derived from its inventor Linux Torvalds. Torvalds was a student at the University Of Helsinki, Finland in early 1990s when he wrote the first version of an UNIX – like kernel us a toy project. He later posted the code on the internet and asked Programmers across the world to help him build it into a working system. The result was Linux. Torvalds holds the copyright but permits free distribution of source code. That is, he overseas development of kernel and owns its trademark. When someone submits a change or a further enhancement, Torvalds and his core team of kernel developers review the merit of adding it to kernel source code. Some popular operating systems are UNIX, MS – DOS, Microsoft windows, Microsoft Windows NT, and Linux.

1.4. Operating Systems

1.4.1. Mainframe Operating Systems

At the high end are the operating Systems for the mainframes, those room- sized computer still found in major corporate data centres. These computers distinguishes themselves from personal computers in terms of their I/O capacity. A mainframe with 1000 disks and thousands of gigabytes of data is not unusual; a personal computer with these specifications would be odd indeed. Mainframes are also making something of a comeback as high–end web servers, servers for large–scale electronic commerce sites, and servers for business–to–business transactions.

The operating system for Mainframes are heavily oriented towards processing many jobs at a time, most of which need prodigious amounts of I/O. These are typically three kinds of services: batch, transaction processing and time sharing. A batch system is one that process routine jobs without any interactive user present. Claims processing is an insurance company or sales reporting for a chain of stores is typically done in batch mode. Transaction processing system handles large number of small requests. Time sharing system allows multiple remote users to run job on the computer at once such as querying a big database. An example of mainframe operating system is OS/390, a descendant of OS/360.

1.4.2. Server Operating Systems

One level down are the server operating systems. They run on servers, which are either very large personal computers, workstations, or even mainframes. They serve multiple users at once over a network and allow the users to share hardware and software resources. Servers can provide print services, File services or web services.

Internet providers run many server machines to support their customers and web sites use servers to store the web pages and handle the incoming requests. Typical server operating systems are UNIX and Windows 2000. Linux is also gaining ground for servers.

1.4.3. Multiprocessor Operating Systems

An increasingly common way to get major–league computing power is to connect multiple CPUs into a single system. Depending on precisely how they are connected and what is shared, these systems are called Parallel Computers, multicomputer or multiprocessors. They need special operating Systems, but often these are variations on the server operating system, with special features for communication and connectivity.

1.4.4. *Personal Computer Operating Systems*

The next category is the personal computer operating system. Their job is to provide a good interface to a single user. They are widely used for word processing, spread sheets, and internet access. Common examples are windows 98, windows 2000, the Macintosh operating system, and Linux. Personal computer operating systems are so widely known that probably little introduction is needed. In fact, many people are not even aware of other kinds exist.

1.4.5. *Real–Time Operating Systems*

Another type of operating systems is the real–time system. These systems are characterized by having time as a key parameter. For example, in industrial process control systems, the real–time computers have to collect data about the production process and use it to control machines in the factory, often there are hand dead–lines that must be met. For example, if a car is moving down an assembly line, certain actions must take place at certain instants of time. If a welding robot wields too early or too late, the car will be ruined. If the action absolutely must occur at a certain moment (or within a certain range) we have a hard real–time system. Another kind of real–time system, in which missing an occasional deadline is acceptable. Digital audio or multimedia systems fall in this category. Vxworks and QNX are well–known real–time operating systems.

1.4.6. *Embedded Operating System*

Continuing on down to smaller and smaller systems, we come to palmtop computers and embedded systems. A palmtop computer or PDA (Personal Digital Assistant) is a smaller computer that fits in a shirt pocket and performs a small number of functions such as an electronic address book and memo pad. Embedded systems run on the computers that control devices that are not generally thought of as computers, such as TV sets, microwave ovens, and mobile telephones. These often have some characteristics of real–time systems but also have size, memory, and power restrictions that make them special. Examples of such operating systems are Palm OS and Windows CE (Consumer Electronics).

1.4.7. *Smart card Operating Systems*

The smallest operating systems run on smart cards, which are credit card sized devices containing a CPU chip. They have very serve processing power and memory constraints. Some of them can handle only a single function, such as electronic payments, but others can handle multiple functions on the same smart card. Some smart cards are Java oriented. What this means is that the ROM on the smart cards hold an interpreter for the Java virtual Machine (JVM). Java applets are downloaded to the card and are interpreted by the JVM interpreter. Some of these cards can handle multiple java applets at the same time, leading to multiprogramming and the need to schedule them. Resource management and protection also become an issue when two or more applets are present at the same time. These issues must be handled by the operating system present on the card.

1.5. Computer Hardware Review

1.5.1. Processors

The brain of the computer is the CPU. It fetches instructions from memory and executes them. The basic cycle of every CPU is to fetch the first instruction from memory, decode it to determine its type and operands, execute it, and the fetch, decode, and execute subsequent instructions. In this way, programs are carried out.

In addition to the general registers, which is used to hold variables and temporary results, most computers have several special registers that are visible to the programmer. One of these is the Program Counter, which contains the memory address of the next instruction to be fetched. After the instruction has been fetched, the program counter is updated to point to its successor.

Another register is the stack pointer which points to the top of the current stack in memory. The stack contains one frame for each procedure that has been entered but not yet exited.

Yet another register is the PSW (Program Status Word) this register contains the condition code bits, which are set by comparison instructions, the CPU priority, the mode and various other control bits. User programs may normally read the entire PSW but typically may write only some of its fields. The PSW plays an important role in system calls and I/O.

1.5.2. Memory

The second major component is any computer is the memory. Ideally, a memory should be extremely first, abundantly large, and dirt cheap. No current technology satisfies all of these goals, so a different approach is taken. The memory system is constructed as a hierarchy of layers as shown in the fig.

The top layer consists of the registers internal to the CPU. They are made of the same material as the CPU and are thus just as fast as the CPU. In this, memory is divided into several categories cache, RAM, ROM, EEPROM, and CMOs.

Cache memory, which is mostly controlled by the hardware. Main memory is divided up into cache lines typically 64 bytes, with addresses 0 to 63 in cache line 0, addresses 64 to 127 in cache line 1, and soon. When the program needs to read a memory word, the cache hardware checks to see of the line needed is in the cache. If needed it is, called a cache bit, the request is satisfied from the cache and no memory request is sent over the bust to the main memory. Cache memory is limited in size due to its high cost. Some machines have two or even three levels of cache, each on slower and bigger than the one before it.

RAM is a Random Access Memory, old timers sometimes call it Cory memory, because computers in the 1950's and 1960s used tiny magnetisable ferrite cores for main memory. Currently, memories are ten to hundreds of megabytes and growing rapidly. All CPU requests that cannot be satisfied out of the cache go to main memory.

ROM is a Read Only Memory, which is programmed at the factory and cannot be changed afterwards. It is fast and inexpensive. On some computers, the bootstrap loader used to start the computer is contained in ROM. Also, some I/O cards come with ROM for handling low – level device control.

EEPROM (Electrically Erasable ROM) and flash RAM are also non-volatile, but in contrast to ROM can be erased and rewritten. However, writing them takes orders of magnitude more time than writing RAM, so they are used in the same way ROM is, only with the additional feature that it is now possible to correct bugs in programs they hold by rewriting them in the field.

Yet another kind of memory is CMOS, which is volatile, many computers use CMOS memory to hold the current time and date. The CMOS memory and the check circuits that increments the time in it are powered by a small battery, so the time is correctly updated, even when the computer is unplugged.

1.5.3. I/O Devices

Memory is not the only resource that the operating system must manage I/O devices also interact heavily with the operating system. Normally I/O devices consist of two parts: a controllers and device itself. Controller is a chip or a set of chips on a plug–in board that physically controls the device. It accepts commands from the operating system, for example, to red data from the device, and carries them out. In many cases, the actual control of the device is very complicated and detailed, so it is the job of the controller to present a simpler interface to the operating system. Controller is different software is needed to control each one. The software that talks to a controller, giving its commands and accepting responses, is called a device driver. Each controller manufacture has to supply a driver for each operating system is supports. Every controller has a small number of registers that are used to communicate with it. For example, a minimal disk controller might have register for specifying the disk address, memory address, sector count and direction. To activate the controller the driver gets a command from the operating system, then translates it into the appropriate values to write into the device registers.

1.5.4. Buses

Normally figure has eight buses (cache, local, memory, PCI, SCSI, USB, IDE and ISA). Each with a different transfer rate and function. The operating system must be aware of all of them for configuration and management. The two main buses are the original IBM PC ISA (Industry Standard Architecture) bus and its processor, (successor). The PCI (Peripheral Component Interconnect) bus. The ISA bus, which was originally the IBM PC/AT bus, run at 8.33 MHz and can transfer 2 bytes at once; for a maximum speed of 16.67 MB/sec.

In addition, this system contains three specialized buses: IDE, USB and SCSI. The IDE bus is for attaching peripheral devices such as disks and CD ROMs to the system. The IDE bus is an outgrowth of the disk controller interface on the PC/AT and is now standard on nearly all Pentium–based system for the hard disk and often the CD–ROM. The USB (Universal Serial Bus) was invented to attach all the slow I/O devices such as the keyboard and mouse, to the computer. It uses a small four wire connector, two of which supply electrical power to the USB devices. USB is a centralized bus in which a root device polls the I/O devices every 1 m sec to see if they have any traffic. The SCSI (Small computer System Interface) bus is a high–performance bus intended for fast disks, scanners and other devices needing considerable bandwidth. It can run at up to 160 MB/sec.

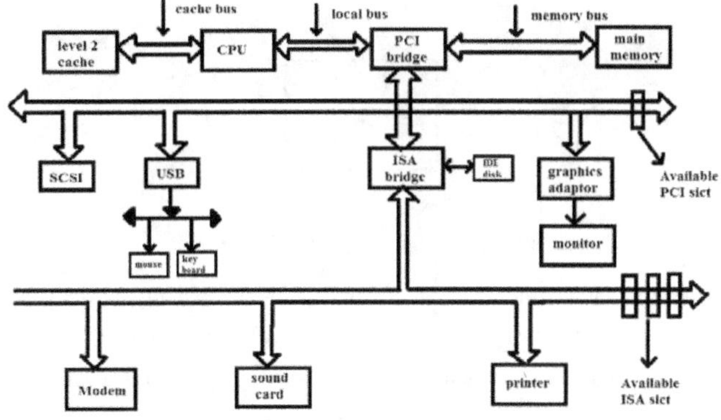

Figure 3: Structure of Large Pentium System

CHAPTER-2

PROCESS MANAGEMENT

Recall that a program that is copied to main memory is called a Job. A Job is also called a Task. A Task is used to refer to a program is execution and the related book keeping information maintained by the operating system. A program is execution is also called a process. A process would require resources like CPU time (to execute the program) memory (to store the program), files (access data) etc. The term Job, task and process are synonymous. The following real world examples of cooking would help in understanding the concept of process better.

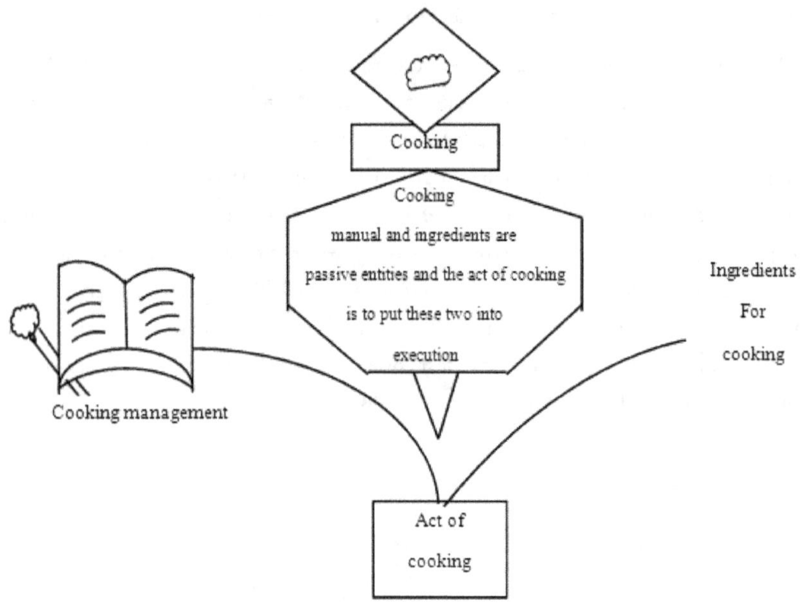

Figure 4: Real World Example for Process

Refer to figure 3 for the following discussion. The cooking manual and all the ingredients for cooking are considered to be passive entities. The act of putting this into action, by cooking, using the cooking manual and the ingredients is the one which produces the desired dish. The program is analogous to the cooking manual and the process (Program in execution) is analogous to cooking. A process requires various resources (like memory, file etc) to execute the program. Process management deals with the various strategies used for managing the different resources which are required for a program to execute. Process management address the following questions.

1) When should a program be brought into main memory?
2) In what way various jobs in main memory is processed?
3) What action should be taken when a job is stopped before its completion?

This section covers some of the fundamental concepts of process management. The various techniques used in process management are introduced with a study on their advantages and disadvantages. The function of process management is to:

1) Keep track of the status of the various process in memory
2) Choose some process for execution based on some criteria.
3) Co-ordinate communication between various process and synchronization between these processes.

2.1. Structure of a Process

Recall from the previous discussion that a program is a set of instructions also called the code and a process is a program in execution. A process maintains information about the contents of the pc and the various registers. A process is said to consist of three regions namely the code region, Data region and the stack region. Refer to the figure for the discussion on stack.

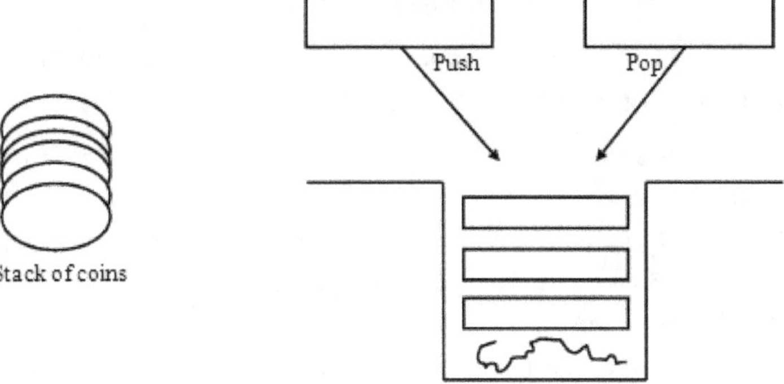

Figure 5: Example of a Stack

A stack is a data structure where the data is removed in the reverse direction in which they are added. So the most recently added data would be the first to be removed. This principle is called Last in First out principle (LIFO). The last element which is added to the collection would be the first to be removed from the collection. Adding an element to the stack is called parhving and removing an element from the stack is called popping. The pile of coins is stored in the last in first out manner. In a stack the elements are added from one side only. Another example for stack is the pile of plates in a during hall which are stored in a last in first out manner. The code region corresponds to the program code. The stack region holds all temporary data and the data region holds all the global data. The word region, segment and section one used interchangeably and mean the same. But why is there a need to distinguish these regions?

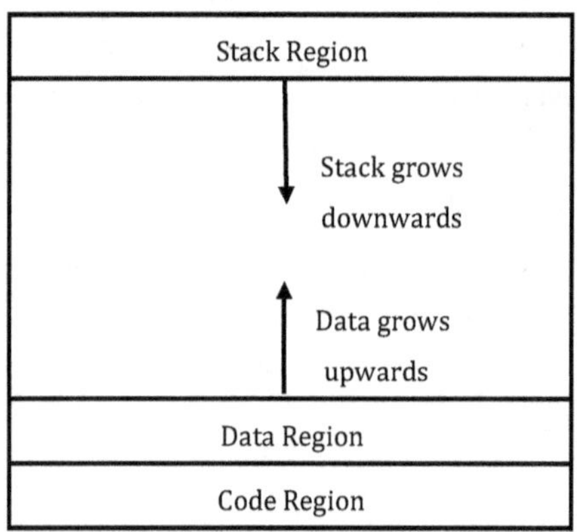

Figure 6: Structure of Process

Refer to figure 5 for the discussion on process structure. A process is divided into various regions for the following reasons.

1) To ensure that there is a level of protection within the different modules of the program
2) To allow sharing of the code for multiple instances of the program, for example, editing multiple word documents at the same time where in the code region for the word editor is shared across these documents.

The stack region is said to group downwards and data region is said to grow upwards. What does this mean?

Whenever a program is being copied into main memory the upper part of the program's memory is reserved to store all local variables. This is the stack region. The process starts by storing data in the stack region from the highest memory address available for the process. The subsequent data which are stored in the region are stored in the next memory address which is available just below the earlier one. This way the stack grows downwards and the data region grows in the other direction which is upwards. This is similar to having the conventional way of writing and the Arabic way of writing in the same line. In the conventional way one starts writing from the left whereas in the Arabic writing one starts from the right most corners. The stack region in the process structured is similar to the Arabic writing and the data region in the process structure is similar to the conventional writing.

2.2.   Process States and States Transitions

Like human begins a process also has life and goes through a cycle called process life cycle. The various states through which a process goes through during a process Life cycle indicates the current status of the process and also provides information on what it is allowed to do next. To understand the life cycle process better consider the following real world examples of a fresh graduate joining a software company and undergoing tramping.

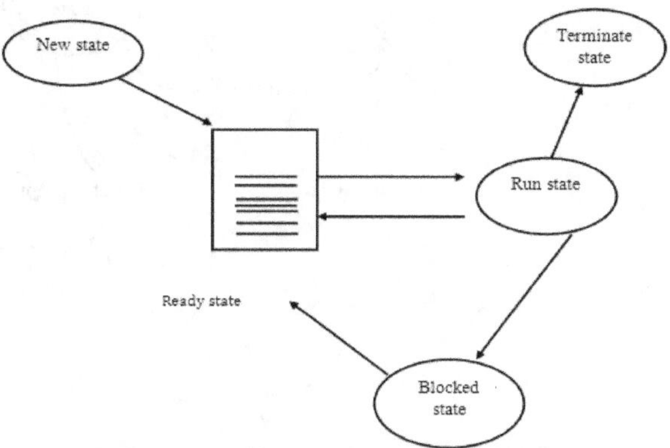

Figure 7: Real World Example for Process Life Cycle

A fresh graduate who is offered a job in a software company is a new state which denotes that he would be new to the industry and to the training. When he joins the company he moves to the ready state which denotes that he is ready for training. In the first week of joining the company where in the software engineer would be spending time finishing all HR formalities would signify the ready state waiting for training. The software engineer would move to the run state when he actually undergoes his training. When he/she absents himself/herself for more than three days during the training he/she moves to the blocked state from where in he/she would be asked to join a new batch of training. This means that the software engineer would be moving from blocked state to ready state. If due to business requirements a trainee is pulled out of tearing then he/she would move from run state to a ready state. A trainee on successful completion of the training moves to a terminate state which denotes the end of this training. In this example the undergoing training is taken as the execution context. The above mentioned states are precisely the various states in which a process can exists during the time of its creation till its completion. In other words a process can be in any one of the following states refer figure)

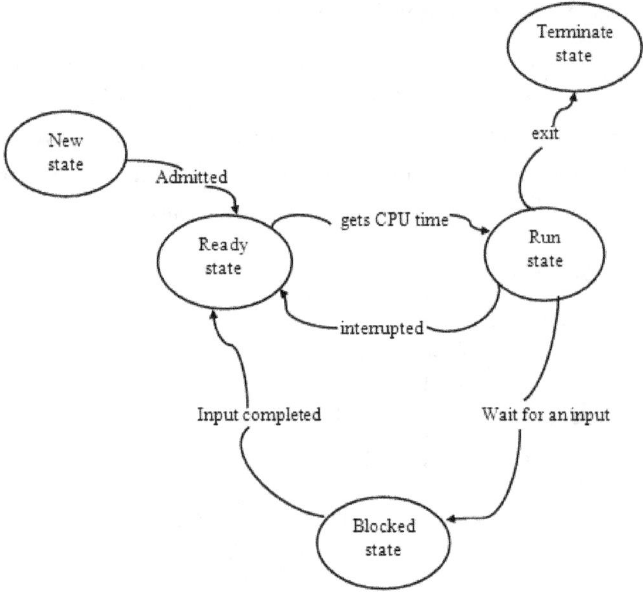

Figure 8: Process States and State Transition

New state: A state where the process is crated and the OS recognizers the process but no resources are allocated to the process.

Ready state: A state where the process is ready for execution and is waiting for the CPU time.

Blocked state: A state where in a running process does not have immediate access to a resources and waiting for some event to occur, like waiting for an input from the keyboard.

Terminate state: A state where the process has finished its execution.

2.3. Multi Process

Multi process can reside in memory and these processes would be in one of the process states mentioned earlier. The process manager maintains different queues for these processes. What kind of relationship do these processes have? Processes are broadly categorized into two based on their interaction with the-other processes. These two categories are discussed below.

Independent Process

An independent process is one which does not affect other processes and neither does it get affected by them. Taking the final examination is an example of the independent process.

Cooperating Process

A cooperating process is one which shares some information or communicates with other processer in order to speed up the computation time. Working on a project as a team is an example of a cooperating process.

2.4. Inter Process Communication

Communication between cooperation processes is called Inter Process Communication (IPC). Cooperating systems (Process) communicated by one or more of the following ways. Sharing a portion of memory among then where in the information to be communicated is put so that the other process can read from there. This mechanism is called shared memory concept. An example of shared memory would be the bulletin board. Passing message across these cooperating processes. This mechanism is called message passing concept. An example of message passing would be the mail application. Sending signals to other processes. This mechanism is called signal processing concept IPC using signals would be used only to convey minimal information. An example for signal processing would be the traffic signal.

2.5. Multiprogramming

The ability of the operating system to have multiple programs in memory which are ready for execution is called multiprogramming. The term multiprogramming is normally associated with a Uni processor system. In both manual loading and batch processing, jobs are loaded into a system and processed on at a time.

Once loaded, a job remains in main memory until its execution is over, and the next job is loaded currently only after the completion of the current job. Figure shows that in such a situation, the currently loaded job that is being executed is the sole occupant of user's area of main memory and has CPU exclusively available for itself. Figure is an illustration of uni programming model in which only one job is processed at a time and all system resources are available exclusively for the job until its completion.

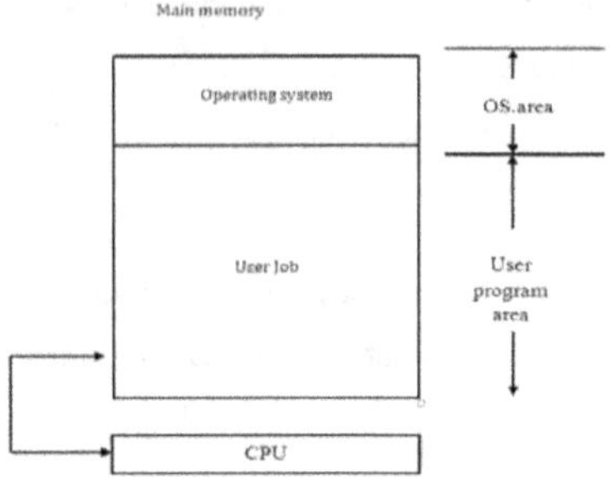

Figure 9 : Uniprogramming System Model

A job doesn't need CPU for entire duration of its processing because in addition to computing it often needs to perform I/O operations during the curse of its processing. In fact, depending on CPU utilization during the course of processing jobs re broadly classified into two types

1) **CPU- Bond Jobs:** These jobs mostly perform computations with little I/O operations. Hence, their CPU utilization is very high. Programs used for scientific and engineering computations usually fall in this category of jobs.

2) **I/O bound Jobs:** These jobs mostly perform I/O operations with little computation. Hence, their CPU utilization is very low. Programs used for commercial data processing applications usually fall in this category of jobs.

In a uniprogramming system, CPU is idle whenever the CPU becomes ideal whenever the job being currently processed performs I/O operations. CPU is idle whenever the job currently processed performs I/O operations. CPU idle time may not be significant for CPU-bound jobs, but it may be of the order of 80-90% for I/O bound jobs.

Multiprogramming is interleaved execution of two or more different and independent programs by a computer. Figure has already introduced the notation of two programs(Operating system and user program) consistent resident simultaneously in main memory of a computer. This concept is carried a step further in Multiprogramming by enabling tow or more user programs to reside simultaneously is main memory and carrying out their interleaved execution with the multiple user programs residing simultaneously in the user program area of main memory, whenever the user program which was executing goes to perform I/O operations, CPU is allocated to another user program in main memory that is ready to use CPU, instead of allowing CPU to remain idle. CPU switches from one program to another almost simultaneously. Hence, in multiprogramming, several user programs share CPU time to keep it busy.

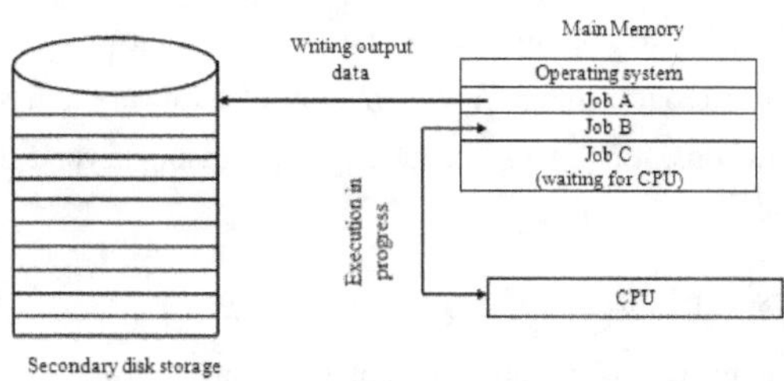

Figure 10: A typical Scenario of Jobs in a Multiprogramming System

Figure shows a typical scenario of jobs in a multiprogramming system. At the time instance shown, there are three user jobs(A,B and C) residing in the memory out of which job A is performing I/O operation (writing to disk) job B is executing (Utilizing CPU time) and Job C is waiting for CPU to become free. Actually, as shown in figure in case of multiprogramming all jobs residing in main memory are in one of the following three states.

1)   Running (it is using CPU)
2)   Blocked (it is performing I/O operations)
3)   Ready (it is waiting for CPU to be assigned to it)

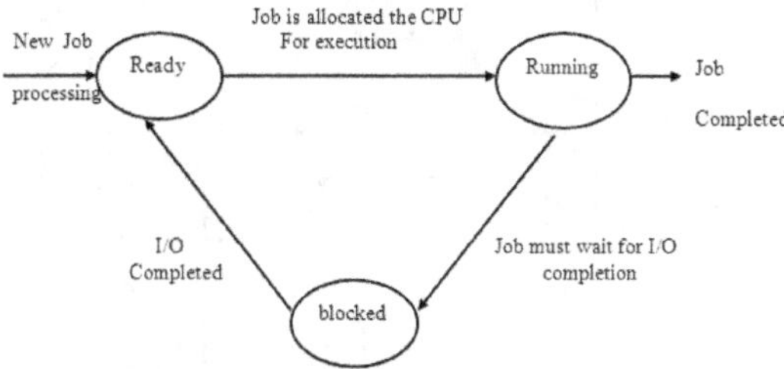

Figure 11: Three Different States of Jobs in Main Memory in a Multiprogramming System

Requirements of Multiprogramming Systems

Multiprogramming systems have better throughput than uniprogramming systems because CPU's idle time is reduced drastically. However, they are more sophisticated because they require following addition hardware and software features.

1) Large Memory

Multiprogramming requires large main memory to accommodate a good number of user programs along with operating systems.

2) Memory Protection

Multiprogramming requires a memory protection mechanism to prevent a job from changing another job's program/data. A combination of hardware and software protection mechanism is used for this. It prevents one job from addressing beyond the limits of its own allocated memory area.

3) Job Status Preservation

In multiprogramming, when a running job is blocked for I/O processing. CPU is taken away scheduled from it and given to another job that is ready for execution. The blocked job resumes it execution sometime later. However, this requires preserving the Job's complete status information when CPU is taken away from it and restoring this information back before CPU is given to it again. To enable this, operating system maintains a process control block(PCB) for each loaded process. Refer figure shows a typical process control block.

<table>
<tr><td>Process identifier</td></tr>
<tr><td>Process state</td></tr>
<tr><td>Process counter</td></tr>
<tr><td>Value of various
CPU registers</td></tr>
<tr><td>Accounting and
scheduling information</td></tr>
<tr><td>I/O status information</td></tr>
<tr><td>.
.
.</td></tr>
</table>

Figure 12: A typical Process Control Block (PCB)

4) Proper Job Mix

A proper mix of I/O bound and CPU-bound job is required to overlap the operations of CUT and I/O devices effectively. If all loaded jobs need I/O at the same time, CPU will again be idle.

Hence, jobs resident simultaneously in main memory should contains a good mix of CPU-bound and I/O bound jobs so that at least one job is always ready to utilize the CPU.

5) *CPU Scheduling*

In a multiprogramming system, often there are multiple jobs in ready state. Hence, when the CPU becomes free, operating system must decide which of these ready jobs should be allocated to the CPU for execution. A part of the operating system that take this decision is called CPU scheduler, and the algorithm it uses for this is called CPU scheduling algorithm.

2.6. Multiprocessing

Multiprocessing is simple terms mean multiple process executing simultaneously. The term multiprocessing is normally associated with the multiprocessor system.

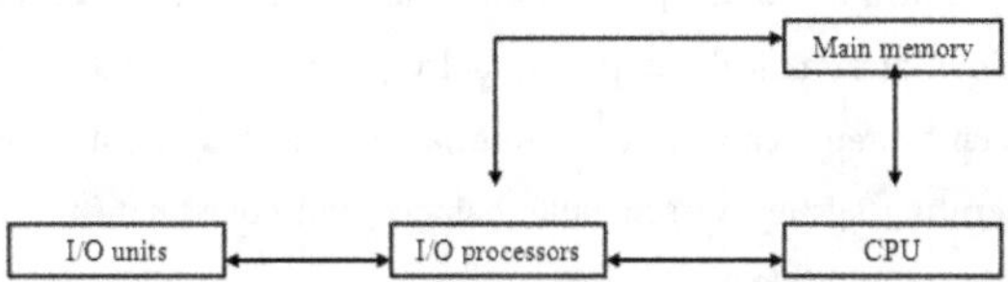

Figure 13: Architecture of a Computer System with its CPU Memory and I/O Processors

The idea of using I/O processor to improve the system performance was carried to a step further by designing system with multiprocessing system because they use multi processor and can execute multi processes concurrently. Multiple CPU's of these systems are used to process either instructions from different and independent programs or different instructions from the same program simultaneously. Figure shows basic organization of a typical multiprocessing systems.

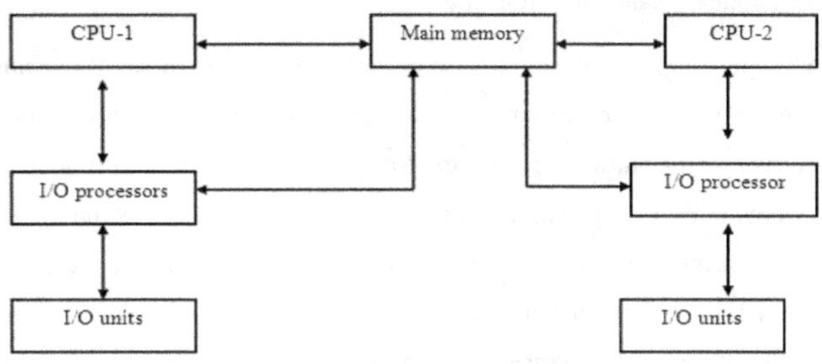

Figure 14: Basic Organization of a Typical Multiprocessing Systems

In general, multiprocessing systems are two types:

1) Tightly coupled system.
2) Loosely coupled system.

In tightly system, there is a single system. Wide primary memory shared by all processors. On other hand, in loosely coupled system, the processors do not share memory and each processor has its own local memory.

Advantages and Limitations of Multiprocessing

Multiprocessing system have the following advantages.

Better Performance

They also have better reliability than single-processor system. In a properly designed multiprocessor system, if one of the processor breaks down, the other processor(s) takes over the system workload automatically until the faulty processor is repaired. Hence, a complete breakdown of such systems can avoided. Multiprocessing system, however, require a very sophisticated operating system to schedule, balance and coordinate the input , output and processing activities of multiple processor.

2.7. Multitasking

The act of switching the processor from one process to another process is called multitasking. i-e multitasking is a result of context switching. In a multitasking system there is only one processor and at a given point of time there is only one program is execution and other programs potentially can run. The ability of the operating system to hold multiple programs in the ready state (to store more than one process) in the memory at a time is called multiprogramming where as the actual act of switching of the processor between these ready jobs based on a policy is called multitasking.

Technically speaking, multitasking is same as multiprogramming. Many authors do not distinguish between. Multiprogramming and multitasking because both refer to the same concept. However, same authors prefer to use the term multiprogramming for multi-user systems (systems that are used simultaneously by many users such as mainframe and server class systems), and multitasking for single user systems(systems that are used only by one user at a time such as a personal completed or a note book computer. Note that even in a single user system often it has multiple tasks being processed by the system. In a multi user system, while multitasking is interleaved execution, of multiple jobs (often referred to as tasks of same user) in a single-user system. Typically computer systems used for such purposes are uniprocessor system (having only one CPU).

2.7.1. Types of Multitasking

The different types of multitasking are

1) Cooperative Multitasking.
2) Preemptive Multitasking.
3) Non-preemptive Multitasking.

Co-operative Multitasking

In this kind of multitasking, which is very primitive, the responsibility for releasing control of the CPU is placed on each and every process that is executing. In this case the process has to voluntarily give up the CPU and normally the CPU is taken up by the process for longer periods of time. A real world example of multitasking co-operative multitasking would be checking into a hotel. There could be many people waiting to book a room (synonymous to CPU time). But the current person who has checked in can continue to stay in this room as long as the he wishes too. Only when the voluntarily checks out the other people would be at toted the room.

Preemptive Multitasking

This kind of multitasking ensures that every process gets a chance to run, preemptive multitasking allows each process to run till it voluntarily relinquishes the CPU or till a fixed duration of time. When the fixed time duration expirees the OS preempts the currently running process. Example is paid parking.

Non-Preemptive Multitasking

In this of multitasking the process which is currently given the CPU time would be allowed to run until it terminates or when its waits for an I/O. Note that difference between cooperative and non-preemptive multitasking. In co-operative multitasking OS, the currently executing process need not relinquish the CPU even when it waits for an I/O. Example: Towing.

How is Multitasking Implemented?

A program called scheduler, which is part of the OS, switches between one processes to another at different instances of time. Whenever a process goes into a blocked state its current context (state information) is saved and the scheduler does a context switch by loading another process for execution. The meeting request in the mail program has a scheduler which helps in viewing the calendar of others.

2.8.   Time Sharing

Time sharing is a mechanism to provide simultaneous interactive use of a computer system by many users in such a way that one feels that he/she is the sole user of the system. It uses multiprogramming with a special CPU scheduling algorithm to achieve this. A time sharing system has many user terminals connected to the same computer simultaneously. Using these terminals, multiple users can work on the system simultaneously. Multiprogramming feature allows multiple user programs to reside simultaneously in the main memory, and special CPU scheduling algorithm allocates a short period of CPU time one-by-one to each user process.

The short period during which a user process gets to use CPU is known as time slice, time slot, or quantum and is typically or the order of 10 to 100 milliseconds. Hence when CPU is allocated to a user process, it users the CPU until the allotted time slice expires, or it needs to perform some I/O operation, or it completes its execution during this period. Notice that CPU is taken away from a running process when the allocated time slice expires. Figure shows the process state diagram of a time sharing system.

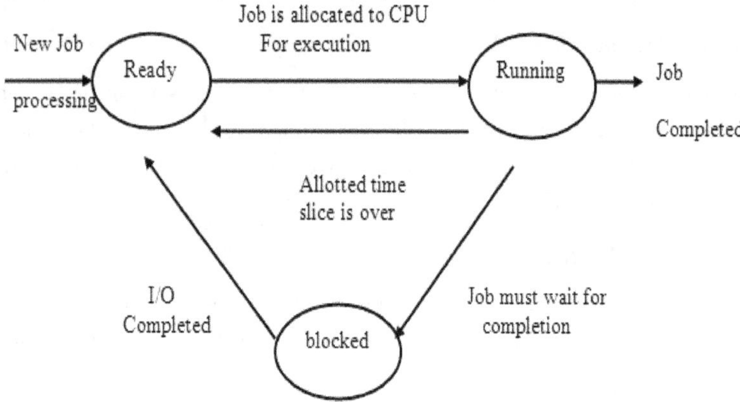

Figure 15: Process State Diagram for a Time-Sharing System

Now let us see how the CPU scheduling algorithm, mentioned above, gives an impression to each user that he/she is the sole user of the system. Let the time slice be 10 milliseconds and the processing speed of the system's CPU be 500 million instruction per second. Hence, the system execute 500 * 10(6)*10(-3)*10=5*10(6)=5 million instructions in 10 milliseconds this is large enough for substantial progress of a single user process.

Requirements of Time-Sharing Systems

Time-sharing systems requires the following additional hardware and software:

1) A number of terminals connected to a system simultaneously, so that multiple users can use the system simultaneously in interactive.

2) Relatively large memory to support multiprogramming.

3) Memory protection mechanism to present a job's instructions and data from other jobs in a multiprogramming environment.

4) Job status preservation mechanism to preserve a job's status information when CPU is taken away from it, and restoring this information back, before CPU is given to it again.

5) A special CPU scheduling algorithm that allocates CPU for a short period one-by-one to each user process in a a circular fashion.

6) An alarm mechanism to send an interrupt signal to CPU after every time slice.

Advantages of Time-Sharing System

Although time-sharing system are complex to design, they provide the following advantages to their users.

1) Reduces CPU Idle Time

A user's thinking and typing speed is much slower than a computer's processing speed. Hence during interactive usage of a system, while a user is engaged in thinking or typing his/her input, a time sharing system services many other users. Hence time sharing systems help in reducing CPU's idle time and in turn, provides increased system throughput.

2) Provides Advantages of Quick Response Time

The special CPU scheduling algorithm used in time sharing systems ensures quick response time to all users.

This feature helps in improving programmer's efficiency by making interactive programming and debugging much simpler and quicker.

3) Offers Good Computing Facility to Small Users

Small users can gain direct access to more sophisticated hardware and software than they could otherwise justify or afford. In time-sharing systems, they merely pay a fee for resources used and are relieved of hardware, software and personnel problems associated with acquiring and maintaining their won installation.

2.9. Threads

A thread is a basic limit of execution. a thread is a single sequential flow of control within a program.

A thread is also known as a light weight process. A process can have May threads of execution.

What Structure Does the Threads Have?

Recall that a process is a program in execution and the process structure is divided into code region, data region and stack region. The code region and data region of a process are shared across different threads of the same process (Refer to figure).

Each thread of a process has it own stack region and PC.

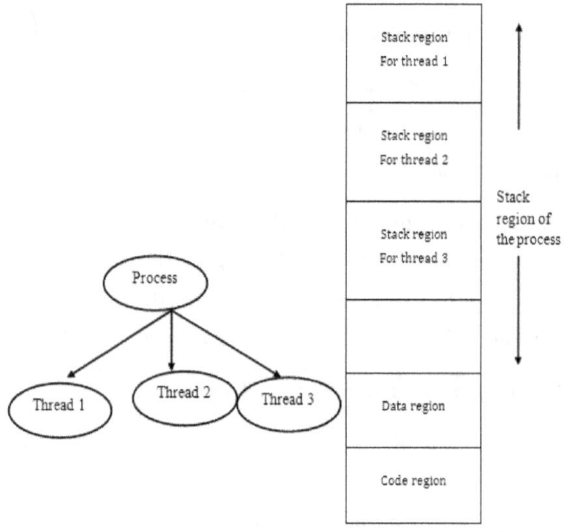

Figure 16: Thread Structure

Why is there a Need for Multiple Threads in a Process?

Consider the following real world example of a editing a document using an editor. This editing would be executed as a thread in the process. Suppose that the user also wants to use the spell check facility available with the editor. If the OS allows only one thread for each process(Single threading) then the user should first finish editing the document and then use the spell check facility.

This would be time consuming and also during ht course of editing the CPU could be idle most of the times. Allowing multiple threads to executes concurrently in the case would improve the CPU utilization and also the spell check can be done as and when the document is edited. Figure indicates(illustrates).

Multithreading concept in the word editor. The spell checked runs consequently as and when the user edits the document. Another good example for multithreading would be the web browsers. As the browser fetches a document it will also concurrently allow the user to interact with the existing information in the browser.

Advantages of Multithreading

1) Multiple threads in a process share the same memory address space. This means memory utilization would be bettered by using multithreading.
2) Concurrent execution of threads would result in faster execution of the process.

2.10. Scheduling

The basis for multitasking is scheduling. Determining when a process is to be run, with in a multitasking environment is called scheduling. When a computer is multi programmed, it frequently has multiple processes competing for the CPU at the same time. This situation occurs whenever two or more processes are simultaneously in the state.

If only one CPU is available, a choice has to be made which process to run next. The part of the operating system that makes the choice is called the scheduler and the algorithm it uses is called the scheduling algorithm. These topics form the subject matter of the following sections.

CPU Utilization

This gives a measure of what percentage of the CPU is being utilized. A scheduling algorithm should be chosen such that the CPU utilization is high.

Throughput

This measure indicates the number of processer executed per unit of time. A good scheduling algorithm is one which has a higher throughput.

Turnaround Time

This is a measure which gives the amount of time taken by a process for its execution. This includes the time spend by the process waiting for main memory, time spend waiting in the ready queue, time spend in executing on the CPU and the time spend doing an I/O. A good scheduling algorithm is one which has a lesser turnaround time for processes.

Waiting Time

This is a measure which gives the amount of time spent by the process waiting in the ready queue. This measure does not take into account the time spend in I/O. A good scheduling algorithm is one which reduces the waiting time for a process.

Response Time

The time taken for submission of a process until the first response is called response time. This measure is very useful in interactive computer systems. A good scheduling is algorithm is one where the response time for each process is as least as possible.

2.10.1. Types of Scheduling

Non-Preemptive Scheduling

In non-preemptive scheduling, a process which is allocated to the CPU time will continue to run until it terminates or until it gets blocked due to an I/O request. In this the scheduling process cannot be force dot relinquish the CPU time. An example of non-preemptive scheduling is the First Come First Serve(FCFS) scheduling policy. Here the process is allotted to the CPU time based on the order in which it enters the ready queue. An example of FCFS is the railway reservation counter.

One of the main disadvantages of the FCFS scheduling algorithm is the monopoly of a process. This could mean that a single process might take all of the CPU time without rehnquishing the same. In the railway reservation counter example this would mean that the current person who is booking the ticket might take most of the time of the reservation clerk by enquiring about various trains their availability. Consider the following illustration for FCFS scheduling policy.

Table 1: Illustration for FCFS Scheduling Algorithm

Process	Estimate runtime (in milliseconds)
P1	6
P2	8
P3	7
P4	3

Table shows four process (P1, P2, P3, P4) waiting in the ready queue for the execution. These processes would be executed in the order in which they entered the ready queue.(ie) P1 followed by P2 followed by P3 followed by P4 as shown in the Gantt chart(fig). To find out the efficiency of the FCFS scheduling algorithm, the average waiting time is calculated.

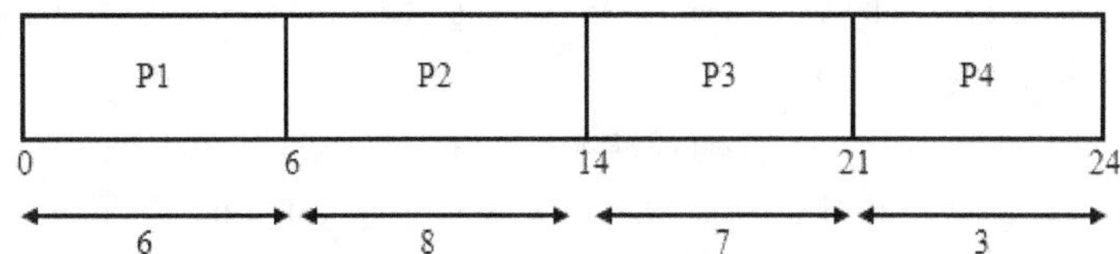

Figure 17: Gantt Chart for FCFS

The waiting time for P1=0 milliseconds

(P1 starts executing first)

The waiting time for P2=6 milliseconds

(P2 starts executing after 1)

The waiting time for P3=14 milliseconds

(P2 starts executing after P1 and P2)

The waiting time for P4=21 milliseconds

(P4 starts executing after P1,P2 and P3)

Hence the average waiting time= (0+6+14+21)/4 = 41/4= 10.25 milliseconds

Turn Around time (TAT) for P1 is=6, P2=14, P3=21, P4=24. Hence the average TAT is= 65/4= 16.25.

The average response time can be calculated as follows : Response time for P1=0, P2=6, P3=14, P4=21. Hence average response time is equal to 10.25 milliseconds. Average Turn Around time can also be calculated as average waiting time + average execution time. So in this example the average waiting time = 7ms and the average execution time = 24/6= 6; Hence average TAT=13ms.

Preemptive Scheduling

In preemptive scheduling the process which is currently running can be removed from the running state by the scheduler, in order to allow another process to run. This act of the scheduler is pre-emption. One mechanism of preemptive scheduling would be to specify a fixed time slice during which a process gets CPU time. If the time slice in 4ms and a process gets its time slice, then another process is given the CPU time. If the original process terminates before 4ms then the CPU will immediately take a context switch which ensures that another process is given the CPU time.

2.10.2. Shortest Job First(SJF) Algorithm Time

The SJF algorithm schedules the processes based on their given estimated run time. The process with the shortest estimated run time would be scheduled first followed by the next shortest and soon. The following real world example (Refer to figure) would help in better understanding of the SJF algorithm.

Consider the scenario where in water needs to be filled in a glass and a bucket from a single tap. Since the glass is of smaller size the water would be filled in the glass first and then followed by the bucket. This is nothing but shortest job first execution. water from the tap is similar to the CPU and the act of filling in water into the glass and bucket are similar to two different processes. Consider the following illustration for SJF algorithm.

Table 2: Illustration for SJF Algorithm

Process	Estimated runtime in milliseconds
P1	6
P2	8
P3	7
P4	3

The table shows for process(P1,P2,P3 and P4) waiting in the ready queue for the execution these processes would be executed based on their estimated run time. The process with the least estimated run time requirement would be executed first followed by the next least and soon. I-e P4 followed by P1 followed by P3 followed by P2 as shown in the Gantt chart in

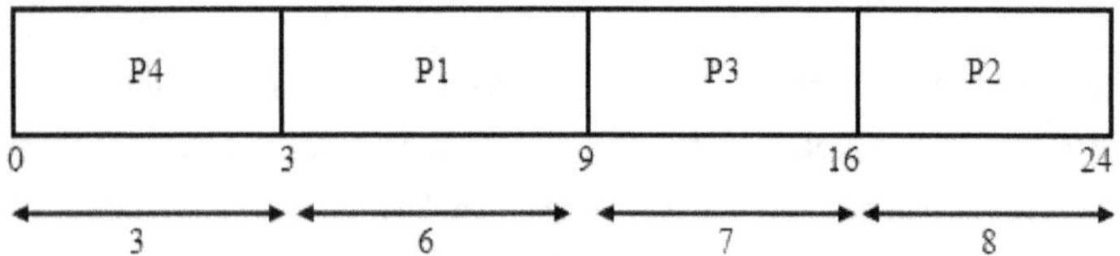

Figure 18: Gantt Chart for SJF Example

The average waiting time for the four processes when the SJF algorithm is used is calculated as follows:

The waiting for P4=o milliseconds

(P4 starts executing first)

The waiting time for P1=3 milliseconds

(P1 starts executing after P4)

The waiting time for P3=9 milliseconds

(P3 starts executing after P4 and P1)

The waiting time for P2=16 milliseconds

(P2 starts executing after P4, P1 and P3)

Hence the average waiting time $\qquad = (0+3+9+16)/4$

$$= 28/4$$

$$= 7 \text{ milliseconds}$$

Accordingly the average TAT will be

$$52/4=13 \text{ milliseconds(better than FCFS)}$$

Average response time is calculated as follows:

P1=3; P4=0; P3=9;P2=16. Hence average response time = 28/4= 7 milliseconds, which is much better than FCFS. In general SJF scheduling algorithm is better than FCFS scheduling algorithm as the average waiting time is less for SJF scheduling algorithm. The key point to note in SJF scheduling algorithm is that by moving the shorter process before a longer process. The waiting time of the shorter process decreases more than the increase in the waiting time for the longer process.

What if a new process (P5 with CPU time as 2ms) arrives into the ready queue when P1 which is currently being executed using the SJF scheduling algorithm has finished 1ms it CPU time i-e at 4th instance of time.

The SJF scheduling algorithm could either be preemptive or non-preemptive scheduling algorithm. If SJF scheduling algorithm is non-preemptive then as soon as P1 terminates P5 is scheduled.

Normally there are two categories of jobs that get into the ready queue. First category is that of the CPU sound jobs and the other category is that of the I/O bound jobs. CPU bound jobs are those which take a lot of CPU time but spend very less time in doing the I/O operations. On the other hand I/O bound jobs are those which take very less CPU time, but spend a lot of time doing I/O operations like printing, receiving input from the keyboard etc. if there are two processes in the ready queue, one being CPU bound and the other one being I/O bound, the I/O bound process which takes less CPU time could be preferred to be executed first and released to do its I/O operation.

This would result is lesser average waiting time. If SJF scheduling algorithm is preemptive then the scheduler checks whether the CPU time of P5 is shorter than what is the remaining of the total estimated time of the currently executing process P1. P1 has still 5ms of CPU time left over. Since P5's CPU time is shorter P1 is pre-empted before it could complete its execution and P5 is executed as shown in figure. In such case, the average waiting time would become

$$(0+3+0+2+11+18)/5=34/5=6.5 \text{ ms}$$

whereas average turnaround time would be

$$(3+(6-4)+11+18+26/5=60/5=12 \text{ ms.}$$

Preemptive SJF scheduling algorithm is also called as shortest remaining scheduling (SRT) algorithm.

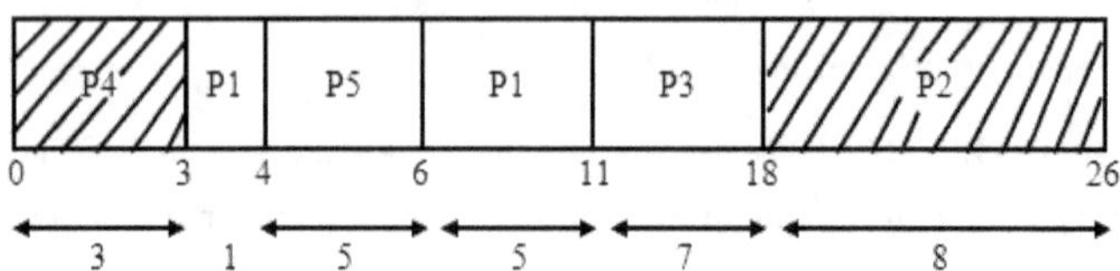

Figure 19: SJF Scheduling Algorithm

The main disadvantage of SJF scheduling algorithm is that more often it is difficult to know the next shortest process in the ready queue, as new processes keep entering the ready queue. also process which requires more CPU time may never get the CPU at all. This is called as starvation or live lock. In the above example, if more and more processes of time duration almost equal to P5 keep entering the ready queue. Then the processes P3,P4 may never get a chance to get executed by the CPU.

2.10.3. Round Robin(RR) Algorithm

The RR algorithm is primarily designed for operating systems where multiple users use the CPU time in such a way that every users feels that they have the whole computer for themselves. Such systems are called time sharing systems. The RR scheduling algorithm is similar to FCFS scheduling algorithm, except for the fact that the pre-emption is added to switch between the processes. In this scheme, a time slice is defined the ready queue is considered to be a circular queue. The scheduler goes around the ready queue, allocating the CPU to each process for a time interval up to 1 time slice.

Recall that a queue works on the principle of First in First Out (FIFO). New processes are added to the other end of the ready queue. The scheduler picks the first process from the read queue and schedules it for execution.

Now If the process terminates before the elapse of the time slice, then the process itself will release the CPU voluntarily. The scheduler will now proceed to next process in the ready queue. On the contrary if the process does not finish to execution during its allotted time slice then a context switch is done by the OS and the next process in the ready queue will be executed. This incomplete process which was pre-empted would be put at the other end of the queue.

The advantage of RR scheduling algorithm is that it ensures every process gets a fixed amount of CPU time unlike FCFS algorithm where there could be process waiting for CPU time for quite a long time. Calculate the average waiting time with respect to Round Robin scheduling with time slice=3 for the processes as shown in

Table 3: Process to be Scheduled

Process	Estimated runtime (in milliseconds)	Arrival time
P1	12	0
P2	10	0
P3	4	1
P4	10	4
P5	12	2

Solution

Refer figure   The Average waiting time is calculated as follows:

Waiting time for P1   = 0+(15-3)+(28-18)+(40-31)

                    = 31

P1	P2	P3	P5	P4	P1	P2	P3	P5	P4	P1	P2	P5	P4	P1	P2	P5	P4

Figure 20: Gantt Chart for Round Robin Scheduling

Waiting time for P2   =   3+(18-6)+(31-21)+(43-34)

                                   =   34

Waiting time for P3   =   (6-1)+(21-9)

                                   =   17

Waiting time for P4   =   (12-4)+(25-15)+(37-28)+(47-40)

                                   =   34

Waiting time for P5   =   (9-2)+(22-12)+(34-25)+(44-37)

                                   =   33

Hence average waiting time is equal to (31+34+17+34+33)/5=29.8 milliseconds. Note that P3 arrives at instance 1. Accordingly for the first slice the waiting time is (b-1). The rest of the calculation is self explanatory. Calculating the average turnaround time and response time is left as an exercise. The disadvantage of RR scheduling algorithm is the overhead involved in maintaining the time slice information for every process which is currently being executed.

2.10.4. Priority Scheduling

In priority scheduling, each process is assigned a priority number which indicates the rating of these processes when compared to each other. This number is used in deciding which process should be scheduled. Consider the following real world examples of vehicles moving in a road(refer to figure) compared to other vehicles on the road an ambulance has a higher priority. Whenever an ambulance comes on a road all other vehicles need to give way for the ambulance because of its higher priority. Similarly in priority scheduling the process with the highest priority is selected for execution. priority scheduling can be either preemptive or non-preemptive.

In preemptive priority scheduling whenever a higher priority process arrives the currently executing process is pre-empted and the new process is assigned to the CPU time. The ambulance example mentioned. In figure is an example for pre-emptive priority scheduling. Calculated the Average waiting time with respect to priority based preemptive scheduling(Assume priority 0 is greater than 1). In case of any tie, use FCFS.

Table 4: Process to be Scheduled

Process	Estimated machine(in milliseconds)	Arrival time	Priority
P1	12	0	2
P2	10	0	1
P3	4	1	0
P4	10	4	2
P5	12	2	1

Average waiting time= 14 Refer Figure for explanation.

The Average Waiting time= (26+(0+4)+0+(38-4)+(14-2))/5=76/5=15.2 milliseconds and the turnaround time will be=24.8 milliseconds

0	1	5	14	26	38	48

Figure 21: Gantt Chart for Priority Based Preemptive Scheduling

In a non-preemptive priority scheduling the current executing process is not disturbed whenever a new higher priority process arrives. This higher priority process is placed at the beginning of the ready queue so that it could be scheduled for execution as soon as the currently execution process terminates.

Disadvantage

The main disadvantage in priority scheduling is that it can cause a lower priority process to wait in the ready queue for an indefinite time hence cawing starvation. One solution to this problem is to slowly increase the priority of a process which is waiting in the ready queue for a longer time. This will ensure that the low priority process will also eventually get executed as its priority would increase gradually. This technique increase the priority of processes which is waiting in the ready queue for a long time called aging.

Chapter-3

Memory Management

To Keep the CPU utilization as high as possible several processes should reside in the main memory. This means that the memory is shared among several competing processes. This necessitates a memory management technique which is capable of handling several processes in the memory. In this chapter we study different algorithms and techniques to achieve the same. The main functions of memory management routines are as follows.

1) Track the status blocks of memory.
2) Determine allocation policy for memory when there is a request.
3) Allocate memory using allocation techniques and update the allocation information.
4) Adopt allocation techniques to free – up memory and update the de allocated memory information.

3.1. Uniprogramming Model

Uniprogramming model is used in systems that process only one ob at a time, and all system resources are available exclusively for the job until it completes. In this memory management scheme one part of the memory is used by operating system and its remaining part is available for use entirely by the currently active user process (see figure 3.1).

The operating system loads a program from disk into the user area of memory and executes it. When the process finishes, it cleans up the user area of memory and the loads the next program to be executed. Although this memory management scheme is simple and easy to implement, it does not lead to proper utilization of main memory resources. This is because the unoccupied memory space in user area (marked unused in the figure) remains unused for entire duration of execution of the currently active user process. Hence, this memory management scheme is now used in very small dedicated computer systems only (systems used for a specific application only).

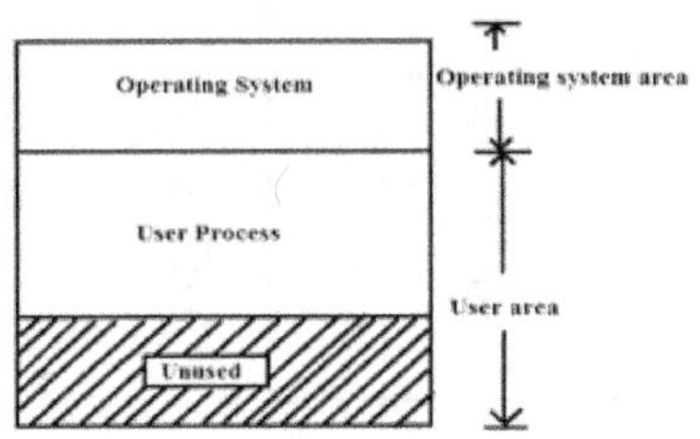

Figure 22: Uniprogramming Memory Model

3.2.   Multiprogramming Memory Models

In a Multiprogramming system, multiple user process need to reside simultaneously in the main memory.

The two memory management schemes used to facilitate this are multiprogramming with fixed number of memory partitions and multiprogramming with variable number of memory partitions. They are described below.

Multiprogramming with Fixed Number of Memory Partitions

In this scheme, the user area of memory is divided into a number of fixed – sized partitions. These partitions may be of same or different sizes, but the size of each partition is fixed. Figure shows a multiprogramming memory model with n equal–sized partitions. Each partition may contain exactly one process. Hence, the number of partitions bounds the degree of multi-programming. That is, at a time only n Processes can be loaded in a system with n memory partitions. All new Jobs are queued in an input queue. When a partition is free, the job from the input queue is loaded into that partition. When a Process terminates, the partition occupied by it comes free for use by another Process. Note that in a system that uses partitions of different sizes, when a partition becomes free, the first process in input queue that fits in it could be loaded into this partition. This scheme of memory management was used in IBM OS/360 mainframe systems for several years. It was called MFT (Multiprogramming with a fixed number of tasks). It is not longer in use.

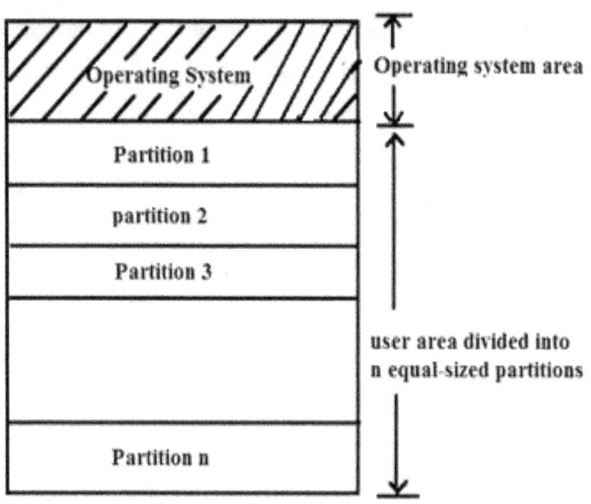

Figure 23: Multi programming Memory Model

Multiprogramming with Variable Number of Memory Partitions

In the scheme described above, since all partitions are of fixed size, any space in a partition that is in excess of actual memory requirement of the process loaded into it remains unused. On an average 50% of memory may remain unused due to this, resulting in under utilization of memory resource. To overcome this problem, another scheme with variable number of memory partitions was introduced. In this scheme, number, sizes and locations of partitions vary dynamically as processes enter and exit the system.

Figure illustrates this memory management scheme with an example, initially, all memory in user area is available for user processes. When a Process enters the system, the memory needed by it is only allocated to it, keeping the rest available for future requests. As processes enter and exit, memory partitions are allocated and de – allocated, each partition being equal to the size of memory required by the process to which it is allocated. Since memory requirement of different processes is generally different, as processes enter and exit, various sizes of free memory blocks are created in memory. Operating system maintains a table to keep track of free memory blocks. When a new process arrives, it searches for a free block that is large enough for this process. If the free block is too large, it is split into two parts.

One part is large enough to be allocated to the process, while the other part that contains remaining memory is entered as a smaller free block in the free blocks table. When a process terminates, it releases the partition allocated to it. The released partition is entered as a free memory block in the free blocks table. However, if the released partition is adjacent to any free block/blocks, it is merged with it to create a large free block, and the associated entries in the free blocks table are updated properly. In this manner, number, sizes and locations of partitions vary dynamically as processes enter and exit the system.

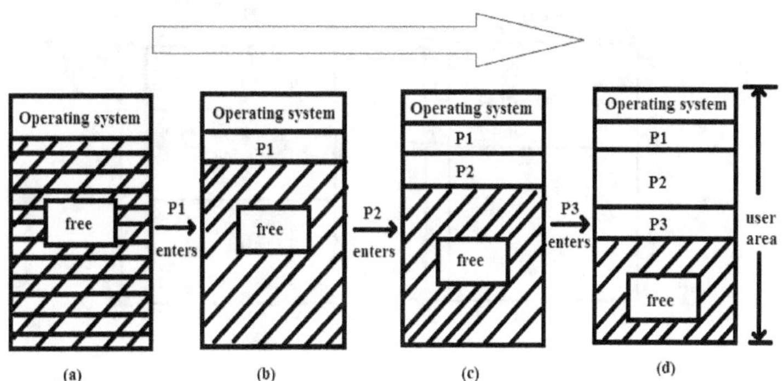

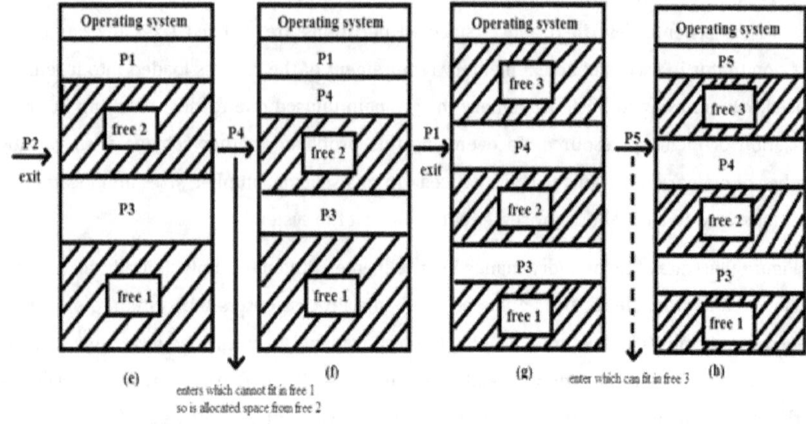

Figure 24: Multi Programming Memory Model Example

3.3. Single Contiguous Memory Allocation

In single contiguous allocation, the user's job is assigned the complete control of the CPU until the job completes or an error occurs. During this time, the user's job is the only program which would reside in memory apart from the operating system. The single contiguous memory management scheme does not require any special hardware. It is generally used in PCs or small workstations with simple batch operating system. This type of operating system does not have multiprogramming facility and there exists one–to–one correspondence between the user and the operating system itself. The various possibilities when single contiguous memory allocation technique is used are highlighted in figure.

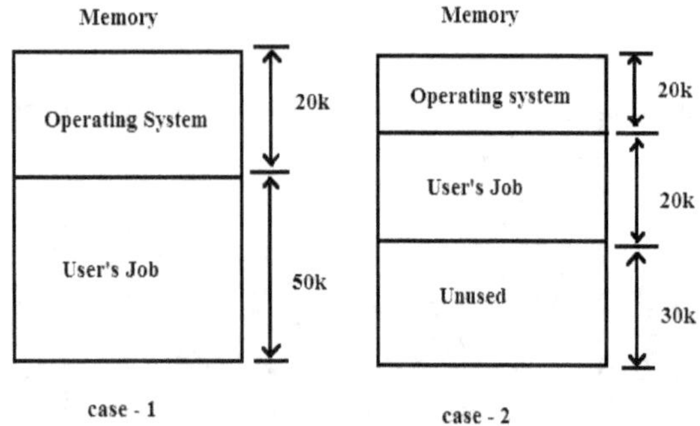

In this memory size is 70k. Here case 1 denotes a scenario where is the user's jobs occupies the complete available memory, the upper part of the memory is however, reserved for the OS program.

In case 2, 30k of memory is free but the new Job cannot be put in memory because of the single contiguous allocation technique. From the above figure and the related discussion, the following advantages and disadvantages of single contiguous allocation technique can be seen.

Advantages

1) It is simple to implement.
2) The operating system takes less space when loaded in memory because of its small size.
3) Provides maximum user area by keeping operating system as well as possible.

Disadvantages

1) Memory is not fully utilized.
2) No support for multiprogramming
3) Poor utilization of processor.
4) Lack of flexibility
5) User address space must be smaller than the physical main memory available
6) Some parts of the memory contain information that is never being accessed.

To overcome these disadvantages, the following memory management techniques are used.

3.4.   Fixed Partition Memory Allocation

In the fixed partitioned memory allocation, the memory is divided into various partitions which of fixed size. This would allow several user Jobs to reside in the memory.

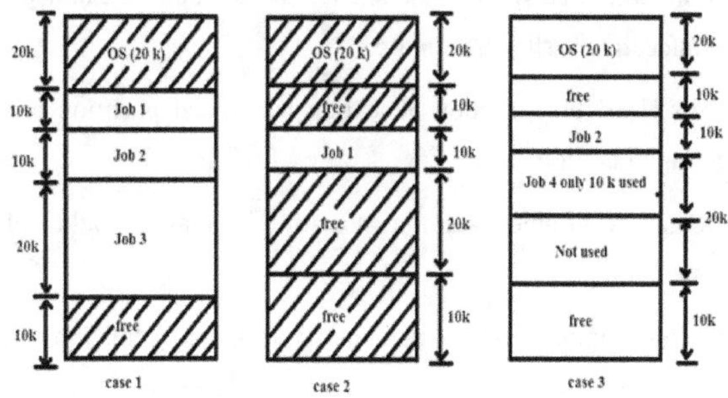

Figure 25: Fixed Partition Allocation

The memory is divided into various partitions of fixed size as shown in figure 3.4. The OS occupies 20k of memory and there are four more portion of size 10k, 10k, 20k and 10k respectively.

In case -1 there are three jobs residing in memory each of which is exactly into the respective partitions. One more partitioned memory is available for a user job. This type of fixed partition allocation supports multiprogramming.

Case -2 suppose that a new Job of size 40k arrives for execution. It can be seen that the total amount of free memory is 40k but the new Job cannot fit into memory for execution because of lack of contiguous free space.

Case -3 this depicts a scenario where Job 4 is allocated a memory Partition of 20k but it has occupied only 10k of this memory partition and the remaining 10k is unused.

Both case 2 and case 3 lead to a scenario where there is free memory available but the same cannot be used for a new Job. This peculiar is called fragmentation of memory. Case 2 leads to external fragmentation wherein there is enough free memory for a new Job but they are not contiguous. Case 3 leads to internal fragmentation where in there is an unused part of memory internal to a memory partition. The advantage of fixed partitioned allocation is to provide multi–programming. Disadvantages of fixed partitioned allocation are internal and external fragmentation of memory. The issue of fragmentation can be resolved in many ways.

Variable Partition Memory Allocation

In this memory management technique there is not pre–determined (fixed) partitioning of memory. Instead this technique allocates the exact amount of memory required for a Job.

As a result of this, the jobs are put in memory in consecutive areas until the entire memory is full or till the remaining free space is too small to accommodate a new Job. An example of variable partition allocation is shown in figure.

The advantage of variable partition allocation over fixed partition allocation is that it prevents internal fragmentation.

The disadvantage of variable partition allocation is that it could still cause external fragmentation of memory.

Suppose that a Job terminates, then the memory occupied by this Job is released and such freed spaces in the memory are called holes. Even though the total free space may be sufficient to accommodate a new Job, there may not be a single large enough hole to accommodate the new Job. This shown in case 2 of figure.25.

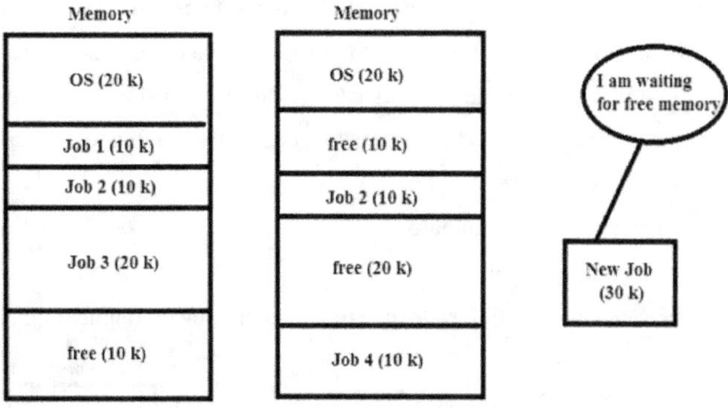

Figure 26: Variable Partition Allocation

Such holes when formed in between the currently executing Jobs, will lead to external fragmentation of memory. Recall that the external fragmentation refers to the wastage of free memory spaces which occur outside the memory space allocated for a Job that is currently being executed. If currently executing Job (Job 2 in case 2 of figure), which is in between the holes, terminates then the holes can be combined to form one big hole. This is called coalescence (merging) of holes.

3.5. Re locatable Partition Memory Allocation

The external fragmentation caused by variable partition memory allocation can be overcome by relocating the currently executing Jobs so that the remaining holes can be combined into one large block of memory. This technique of relocating all occupied areas of memory to one end of the memory so as to get one large block of free memory space is compaction. Figure shows the result of new Job allocated to the memory after compaction. In this technique, the currently executing Job is shifted to one end of the memory, thereby allowing the holes (free spaces) to be combined so that the total available free space is large enough to hold the incoming Job process which was not possible in the previous case. The advantage of Re locatable partition technique is that it is relatively simpler to implement in comparison with the other techniques which address the problem of external fragmentation. Some of the disadvantages of Re locatable partition technique are mentioned below:

1) Relocating the currently executing Jobs afresh would lead to problems in executing instructions that are address dependent (absolute addressing).To address this problem one has to change all the absolute this problem one has to change all the absolute address. This problem doesn't occur in case of relative addressing mechanism.

2) Compaction will have the desired effect of making the total free space more usable for the incoming new Jobs, but is achieved at the expense of large scale movement of the currently executing Jobs. All the Jobs need to be suspended while the re–shuffle takes place. Hence decision has to be made as to when and how often to perform compaction. The memory is compacted:

- As soon as any Job terminates.
- At fixed time intervals.
- When a new Job cannot be loaded into memory due to fragmentation.

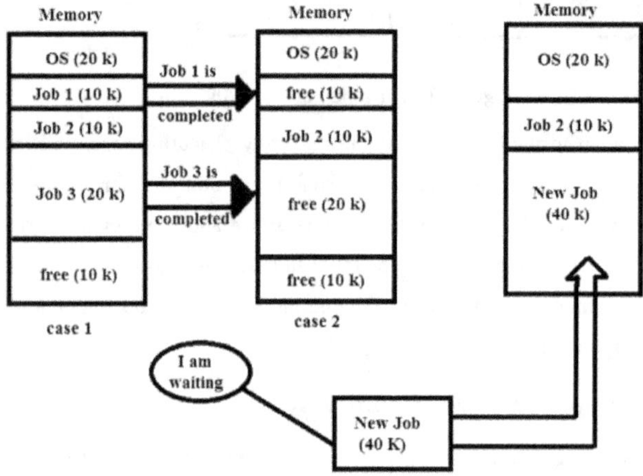

Figure 27: Relocatable Partition Allocation

CHAPTER- 4

DEADLOCK

4.1. Introduction to Deadlock

A set of processes is deadlocked if each process in the set is waiting for an event that only another process in the set can cause. In a multiprogramming environment, several processes may compete for a finite number of resources. A process requests 1 resources; if it is not available at that time, the process enters a wait state. But it may happen that the waiting process will never again change state, because the resources they have requested, are helped by other waiting processes. This situation is called a deadlock.

4.2. Condition for Deadlock

In deadlock, processes never finish executing and system resources are tied up preventing other pending Jobs from starting.

Necessary condition: a dead lock situation can arise, in a system when the following four conditions hold simultaneously in a system.

1) Mutual exclusion condition
2) Hold and wait condition
3) No pre-emption condition
4) Circular wait condition

All four of these conditions must be present for a deadlock to occur. If one of them is absent, no deadlock is possible.

Mutual Exclusion Condition

Each resource is either currently assigned to exactly one process or is available.

Hold and Wait Condition

Processes currently holding resources granted earlier can request new resources.

No Preemption Condition

Resources cannot be pre-empted; that is, a resources can be released only voluntarily by the process holding it, after that process has completed its task.

Circular Wait Condition

There must be a circular chain of the or more processes, each of which is waiting for a resource held by the next member of chain.

4.3.   Dead Lock Modelling

Hold (1972) showed how these four condition can be modelled using directed graph. The graphs have two kinds of nodes: process, shown as circles, and resources, shown as squares. An arc from a resource node(square) to a process node(circle) means that the resource has previously been requested by, granted to, and is currently held by that process.

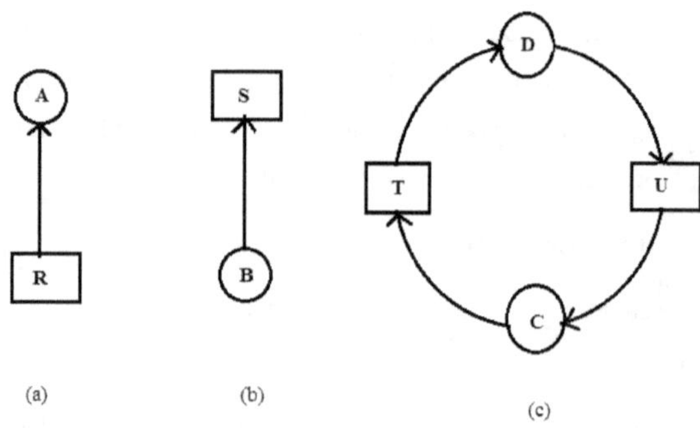

Figure 28: Resource Allocation Graph

In fig 28 (a) resource R is currently assigned to process to a resource means that the process is currently blocked waiting for that the process is currently blocked waiting for that resource. Fig(b) process B is waiting for resource S. Fig(c) we see a deadlock. Process C is waiting for resource T, which is currently held by process D. Process D is not about to release resource T because it is waiting for resource U, held by C. Both process will wait forever.

Now let us look at an example of how resource allocation graph can be used. Dead locks can be described in terms of a direct graph called a System Resource-allocation graph. The graph consist of a set of vertices V and a set edges E. V is partitioned into 2 types

$P = \{ P_0, P_1, \ldots P_n \}$ the set of all the processes in the system. And $R = \{ R_0, R_1, \ldots R_m \}$ the set consist of all resource types in the system.

The directed edge from process Pi to resource type Rj is denoted by Pi→Rj, it signifies that process Pi requested an instance of resource type Rjand is currently waiting for that resource.

A directed edge from Resource type Rjto process P_i, is denoted $R_j \longrightarrow P_i$ it signifies that an instance of resource type R_j has been allocated to process P_j.

A direct edge $P_i \longrightarrow R_j$ is called an request edge; a directed edge $R_j \longrightarrow P_i$ is called an assignment edge.

A requests edge point to only the square Rj, whereas an assignment edge must also designate one of the dots in the square. When a process Pi, requests an instance of resource type Rj, a request edge is inserted in the resource allocation graph.

When this request can be fulfilled the request is instantaneously transformed to an assignment edge. Then the process later releases the resource. The resource-allocation graph below depicts the following situation.

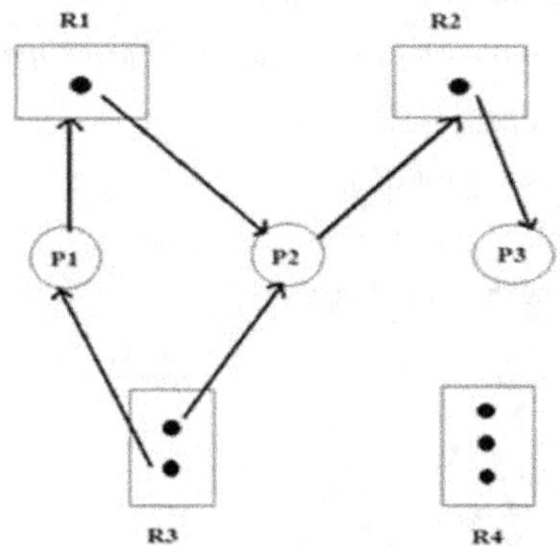

(i) The sets P,R and E:

$$P = \{ P_0, P_1, P_2, \ldots\ldots\ldots P_n \}$$

$$R = \{ R_0,\ R_1,\ldots\ldots\ldots\ldots R_m \}$$

$$E = \{ P_1 \to R_1,\ P_2 \to R_3,\ R_1 \to P_2, R_2 \to P_2, R_2 \to P_1, R_3 \to P_1 \}$$

(ii) Resources Instances

- One instance of resource type R_1.
- Two instance of resource type R_2.
- One instance of resource type R_3.
- Three instances of resource type R_4.

(iii) Process states

- Process P_1 is holding an instance of resource type R_2, and is waiting for an instance of resource type R_1.

- Process P_2 is holding an ₁ₙₛₜₐₙₑₑ of R_1 and R_2, and is waiting for an instance of resource type R_3.
- Process P_3 is holding an instance of R_3.

4.4. Dead Lock Detection and Recovery

In a system where deadlock–prevention or avoidance algorithm are not used, then the system must provide:

1) An algorithm that examines the state of the system to determine whether a deadlock occurred.
2) An algorithm to recover from the deadlock.

4.4.1. *Deadlock Detection with One Resource of Each Type*

If all the resources in a system have only a single instance, then the deadlock detection algorithm can be defined using a variant of the resource allocation graph, called "wait for graph". This graph is obtained from the resource allocation graph by retaining the nodes of resource type and collapsing the proper edges

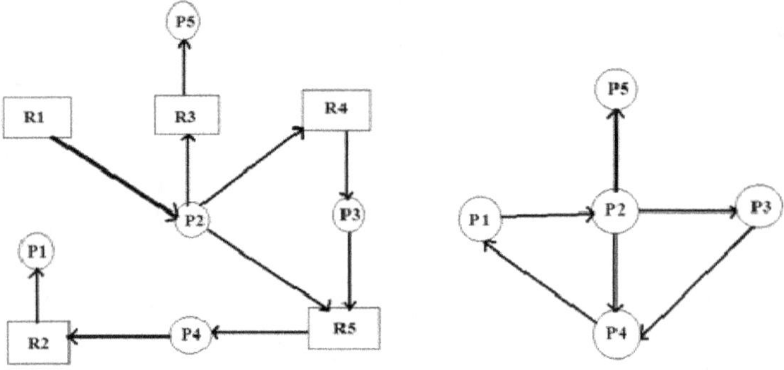

Figure 29: Resource Allocation Graph for Dead Lock

that is an edge from Pi to Pj – in a wait for graph implies that process Pi is waiting for process Pj to release a resource that Pi needs. An edge PiPj ⟶ exists in a wait for graph, if and only if the corresponding Resource allocation graph contains 2 edges PiRq and RqPi ⟶ for some resources ⟶ Rq. Similar to our discussion, a Direct link exists in the system if and only if wait for Graph contains a cycle. Thus to detect a Direct link the system needs a maintain wait for graph and invoke the algorithm periodically which searches for a cycle in the graph.

An algorithm requires an order of N2 operations to detect a cycle in a graph, where 'n' is the number of vertices in the graph.

4.4.2. *Deadlock Detection with Multiple Resource of Each Type*

The above wait for graph is not applicable to resources with multiple instances. This algorithm employs some time varying data structure and is similar to those defined in Banker's Algorithm.

1) Available: A vector of length m indicates the number of resources available in each type.
2) Allocation: An n x m matrix defines the number of resources of each type currently allocated to each process.
3) Request: an n x m matrix indicates the current request of each process. If request $[I,j]$ = k then process P_i is requesting K more instances of resource type R_j.

The detection algorithm checks every possible allocation sequences for the process that is to be completed.

1) Let's work and finish the vectors of length m and n, respectively. Initialize work : = Available. For i=1, 2, ..., n, if allocation i   0, then finish[i] : $\neq$ false; otherwise, finish[j] : + true.
2) Find an index I such that both
   - Finish [i] = false
   - Request :$\leq$work

   if no such i exists, go to step 4.
3) Work := work + allocation i

    Finish[i] : = true

    Goto step 2.
4) Finish[i] = false, for some I, $1 \leq i \leq n$, then the system is in deadlock state. Moreover if finish[i]= false, then process P_i is deadlocked.

This algorithm requires an order of m x n2 operations to detect whether the system is in a deadlocked state.

4.4.3. *Recovery from Deadlock*

Process Termination

Inorder to eliminate a deadlock by aborting a process, the following, one of the two methods can be used. In both of these methods, the system reclaims all the resources allocated to the terminated process.

1) Abort all deadlocked processes.
2) Abort one process at a time until the deadlock cycle is eliminated.

Abort All Deadlocked Process

This method will break the deadlock cycle clearly, but at a greater expense, because the process aborted might have computed for a long time and these partial computation results will have to be discarded and must be probably recomputed later.

Abort one Process at a Time Until the Deadlock Cycle is Eliminated

The methods occurs considerable overhead, since, after each process is aborted, a deadlock – detection algorithm must be invoked to determine whether any processes is still deadlocked. Aborting a process may not be an easy task because if the process is in the middle of file updation, then terminating it in the middle leaves that file in an incorrect state. Similarly if the process is in the middle of the printing data or the printer the system must reset the printer state to a correct state before proceeding with the printing of the next job.

Resource Preemption

In order to eliminate deadlock using resource preemption, pre-empt some of the resources from processes and give them to other processes until the deadlock cycle is broken. If preemption is used in dealing with deadlocks, the following three issues are to be considered.

1) Selection of Victim
   - Which resources and which processes are to be pre-empted.
2) Roll back
   - That is if a resource is pre-empted from a Process, it misses some needed resources, hence, it cannot continue with its normal execution. So, that Process must be rolled back to some safe state and restart it from there.
3) Starvation
   - How do we often ensure the non-occurance of starvation, that is one cannot guarantee that resources will not be pre-empted always from the same Process.

4.5. Deadlock Avoidance

Prevention of deadlocks using previous methods results in low device utilization and reduced system inputs. For avoiding deadlocks, requires additional information about how resources are to be requested. Various Algorithms differ in Amount and type of information requires. One model requires that each process declare the maximum number of resources of each type that it may need. A deadlock avoidance approach, dynamically examines the resource allocation state to ensure that there can never be a circular wait condition. The resource allocation state is defined by the number of available and allocated resources and maximum demands of the processes.

Safe State and Unsafe State

A state is safe if the System is able to allocate resources to each Process. In some order and avoid a deadlock. More formally, a system is in a Safe state only if there exists a safe sequence.

A sequence of Process < P1, P2, ...Pn> is a safe Sequence for the current allocation state if for each Pi, the resources that Pi can still request can be satisfied by the currently available resources plus the resources held by all the Pi with j <i.

In this situation, if the resources that process Pi needs are not immediately available, the Pi needs are not immediately available, the Pi can wait until all of its needed resources, complete its desired took, and return its allocated resources and terminates.

When Pi terminates, Pi can obtain its needed resources and so on. If no such sequence exists, then the system state is said to be unsafe.

A safe state is not a deadlock state. Not all unsafe state are called deadlocks, however, an unsafe state may lead to a deadlock.

As long as the state is safe, the operating system can avoid unsafe states. In an unsafe state, the operating system cannot prevent process from requesting resources such that a deadlock occurs. Behaviour of the process controls unsafe states.

Example: consider a system with 12 magnetic Tape drives and a 3 process: P0, P1, and P2

Process P0 requires – 10 tape drives

Process P_1 requires – 04 tape drives

Process P_2 requires – 09 tape drives

Suppose at time, t_0, P_0 is holding 5 tape drives P_1 is holding 2 and P_2 is holding 2 tape drives.

Maximum needs	Current needs	Available
P_0 10	5	(5 rem + 5 all = 10) =10 rem
P_1 04	2	(3 rem + 2 released = 5) = 5 rem
P_2 09	2	(= 12 – 9 = 03 total)

So at to- system is in safe state sequence < P0, P1, P2> satisfies safety condition. Since, P1 can immediately be allocated all its tape drives and then returns them out of 9 currently allocated, the process P1 can get all its tape drives and return them and finally P2 could get all its tape drives and return them. It is possible to go from a sage state to an unsafe state. Suppose at t1, P2 requests and it is allocated 1 more tape drive, then the system is no longer in a safe state. At this point, only P2 can be allocated all its tape drives. When it returns then the system will have only 4 available tape drives since P0 is allocated 5 tape drives, but has a maximum of 10, it may request 5 more, since they are unavailable, process P0 must wait.

Similarly P2 may request an additional 6 tape drives and will have to wait, resulting in a deadlock. A given safe state avoidance algorithm can be defined to ensure the system will never deadlock.

At $t_1 P_2 = 10$

	Maximum needs		current needs	
P_0	10		5	(4 rem + 5 allocated = 9) - wait
P_1	04		2	(2 rem + 2 allocated = 4) = 4 rem
P_2	09	2+1	2 + 1 (additional request)	
				10 = 12 − 10 = 2 rem

$P_2 = 3$ resource allocated →needs to more to reach maximum, so P_2 also waits.

Banker's Algorithm

A resource allocation graph is not applicable to a resource allocation system with multiple instances of each resource type. The algorithm, which can be used to avoid deadlock in such system, which is less efficient than Resource Allocation Graph algorithm, is Bankers Algorithm.

When a new process enters the system, it must declare the maximum number of instances of each resources type that it may need and this number may not exceed the total number of resources in the system.

When there is a request, the system must determine whether allocation of the resources leaves the system in a safe state. If yes, resources are allocated, otherwise the process must wait until some other process releases enough resources. Several data structures must be defined to implement Bankers Algorithm. These data structures encode the state of the resource–allocation systems. Let 'n' be the number of Processes in the system and 'm' be the number of resources types.

Data structures required are

1) Available

2) Max

3) Allocation

4) Need

Available

A vector of length m indicates the number of available resources of each type. If Available[j] = k, these are k instances of resource type R_j available.

Max

An n x m matrix defines the maximum demand of each process. If Max[i, j] = k, then P_i may request at most k instances of resource type R_j.

Allocation

A n x m matrix defines the number of resources of each type currently allocated to each process. If Allocation [i, j] = k, then process P_i currently allocated k instances of resource type R_j.

Need

An n x m matrix indicates the remaining resource need of each process. If need[i, j] = k, then P_i may need k more instances of resource type R_j to complete its task. Note that Need[i,j] = Max[i,j] – Allocation[i, j].

1) Safety Algorithm

In order to find whether a system is in a safe state, the algorithm can be defined as:

1) Let work and finish be vectors of length m and n, respectively. Initialize work := Available. For i=1,2,,,,,,n, if allocation:≠0 then finish[i]:= false; otherwise, finish[i] := true.

2) Find an i such that both

   - Finish[i] = false
   - $Request_i$ ≤ work.

     If no such I exists, go a step 4.

3) Work : = work + $Allocation_i$

   Finish[i] : = true

   Goto step 2.

4) Finish[i] = true for all I, then the system is in a safe state.

This algorithm may require an order of m x n^2 operations to decide whether the system is in a safe state.

2) Resource – Request Algorithm

Let request I, be the request vector for process P_i. If $request_i$[j] = k, then P_i wants k instances of type R_j. When a request for resource is made by P_i, the following actions are taken.

1) If $request_i$ ≤$need_i$, go to step 2. Otherwise, raise all error condition, since the process has exceeded its maximum claim.

2) If Request < available, go to step 3. Otherwise , P_i must wait, since the resources are not available.

3) Have the system pretenmd to have allocated the requested resources to process P_i by modifying the state as follows:

Available := Available – Request$_i$;

Allocation$_i$:= allocation + request$_i$;

Need$_i$:= Need _ Request$_i$;

If the resulting resource–allocation state is safe, then the transaction is completed and Process P_i is allocated its resources. If new state is unsafe, then P_i must wait for request i and the old resource–allocation state is restored.

4.6. Deadlock Prevention

For a deadlock to occur, each of the 4 necessary condition must hold. By ensuring that at least one of these conditions cannot hold, dead lock occurrence can be prevented.

1) Mutual Exclusion

1) The mutual exclusion condition must hold for non-sharable resources.

2) Sharable resources, do not require mutually exclusive access, thus cannot be involved in a deadlock. Eg: read only files.

In general it is not possible to prevent deadlock, by denying the mutual exclusion condition. Some resources are intrinsically non-sharable.

2) Hold and Wait

In order to ensure hold and wait condition never occurs in the system, a process requesting a resource, should not hold any other resources.

1) One protocol that can be used requires each process to request and be allocated to its resources before its begins execution.

2) Alternative protocol allows a process to request resources only when the process has none.

3) No- Preemption

Attacking the third condition is even less promising than attacking the second one. If a process has been assigned the printer and its in the middle of printing its output, forcibly taking away the printer because a needed plotter is not available is tricky at best and impossible at worst.

4) *Circular Wait Condition*

One way of ensuring this condition never bolds is to impose a total ordering of all resource types and to make the process to request resources in an increasing order of enumeration.

Let $R = (R1, R2, ..., R_n)$ be a set of resource types. Assign each resource type a unique integer number, which is needed in comparing 2 resources to determine whether one preceeds another in the order.

Define a one – to – one function

$F : R \rightarrow N$, where N is a set of natural numbers.

Ex: F (Tape Drive) = 1

F (Tape Drive) = 2

F (Tape Drive) = 15

Now, using the protocol below deadlocks cannot be pre-empted.

1) Each process can request resources only in an increasing order of enumeration.
    a) That is, a Process can initially request any number of instance in a resource type say R_i.
    b) Afterwards, a process can request instances from resources type R_j, if and only if F $(R_j) > F (R_i)$.
    c) If several instance of same resource type is needed, a single request for all of them must be issued.
2) Alternatively, when a Process requests an instance of resource type R_j. It has released any resource R_i such that F $(R_i) \geq F (R_j)$. Using these two protocols, circular wait condition cannot hold.

CHAPTER-5

FILE SYSTEMS

5.1. Files

File is the visible aspect of the operating system. It also provides the means for online storage, as well as access to both data and programs belonging to the operating system and users of the system.

1) A collection of files where each storage corresponds to a related data.
2) A directory structure which organizes files and provides information about all the files in the system.
3) Partitions: These are used to separate logically or physically the large collections of directories.

A file is a collection of related information that is recorded on a secondary storage. A files usually represents programs (some and object) and data. Files may be in free – form like text files or may be formatted rigidly. This information in a file is defined by its creator and will have a defined structure according to its type.

For Example

1) A text – file is a sequence of characters organized into lines or pages
2) A source file is a sequences and functions and so on.

Attributes of a File

A file is named for the user's convenience and is referred to by its name. A name is usually a character string like test.c, test.f,etc. Attributes of a files, vary from one operating system to another but typically the attributes are:

1) Name: This will be usually is human readable form.
2) Type: This information is required in the systems which support different types.
3) Location: This is a pointer to a device and to the location of the file on that device.
4) Size: This gives information about, the current size of the file typically in bytes, words, blocks.
5) Protection: This is access–control information and controls reading, writing, executing and so on.
6) Time, data, user identification: This information is kept for the file's creation, last modification and last use.

5.1.1. File Access Methods

Early operating systems provided only one kind of file access known as the: Sequential Access. In these systems, a process could read all the bytes or records in a file in a file in order, starting at the beginning, but could skip around and read them out of order. Sequential files could be rewound, however, so they could be read as often as needed.

Sequential files were convenient when the storage medium was magnetic tape, rather than disk. When disks came into use for storing files, it become possible to read the bytes or records of a file out of order, or to access records by key, rather than by position.

Files whose bytes or records can be read in any order are called random access files. They are required by many applications E–g: Database management systems.

5.1.2. Operations of a File

A file is an abstract data type. In order to define a file, it is required to consider the operations that can be performed on files. Operating system provides system calls to create, write, read, reposition, delete, and truncate files.

1) File Creation

The steps required for file creation are first, space must be found for the file in a file system. Second, an entry for the new file must be made in the directory as it records the name of the file and the location in the file system.

2) Writing a File

In order to write a file, the user must make a system call specifying both the name of the file and the information to be written onto the file. The system must keep a write pointer to the location in the file, where the next write is to be performed and must be updated whenever a write occurs.

3) Reading a File

In order to perform this operation, a system call specifying the file name and where the next block of the file should be placed in the memory, is used.

4) Repositioning Within a File

This operation does not involve any I/O. It is called as file seek. The directory is searched for the approximate entry and current file position is set to a given value.

5) *Deleting a File*

First, the directory will be searched for the named file order to delete the file. Once found, it releases all the space and erase the directory entry.

6) *Truncating a File*

When the user wants the file attributes to remain the same, but to erase the file contents, instead of deleting and searching the file, the truncation of a file allows all the attributes to remain unchanged except the length.

5.1.3. File Naming

Files are an abstraction mechanism. They provides a way to store information on the disk and read it back later. When a process creates a file, it gives the file name.

When the process terminates, the file continues to exist and can be accessed by the other process writing its name. The exact rules for file naming vary somewhat from system to system, but all current operating system allow strings of one to eight letters as legal file names.

Many operating system supports two part file names, with the two parts separated by a period, as in program C. The part following the period is called file extension and usually indicates something about the file. Some of the more common file extensions and their meanings are shown below:

Extension	Meaning
file. bak	Back up file.
file. C	C source program
file. gif	CompuServe graphical Interchange Format Image.
file. h/p	Help file.
file. html	World wide web hyper text mark-up language document
file. JPEG	Still picture encoded with the JPEG standard
file. O	File object (compiler, output).
file. pdf	Portable document format file.
file. ps	Post script file.
file. txt	General text file.
file. zip	Compressed archive.

5.1.4. File Types

In designing a file system and the entire operating system, one must consider whether the operating system must recognize and support the file types. One common approach used for implementing file types name.

Hence the file name is split into two parts

1) Name.

2) Extension, separated by a period.

Character as shown blow

File types	Extension	Function
Source code	.Pas, .C, .p, .ftt, etc	Source code in different Languages.

File types	Extension	Function
Object code	.obj, .o	Compiled, machine Languages not linked.

File types	Extension	Function
Executable	.exe, .com, .bin and so on	Really to run machine Languages program.

Figure 30: Characters

5.2. File System Management

The part of the operating system that deals with effective information management is called as file system management. The term file is used for anything that is stored in the secondary storage. A file could be a program, text files, word documents, image files, audio/video files etc. The file system management of the os deals with management these files and in providing a consistent mechanism for the user to access these files. The desirable feature of a file system are as follows:

1) Provide minimal input and output operation on the files to access the information stored in them.

2) Isolate the differences between the actual physical storage of these files and the one which the end user sees when he/she accesses these files.

The file system management of two well known file system, namely MS-DOS file system and UNIX file system, are discussed in this section.

5.2.1. MS-DOS File System

The file naming convention in DOS consists of logical drive, path and files name. The following examples would help in better understanding of above mentioned terms. Consider the following example shown in Figure suppose that JSC.doc is a file which is placed in a particular location, say C:|JSC |course material. Then c: refers to the logical drive name and C:|JSC | course material is called the path name. The path specifies the location in the logical drive where in the files is present. The path could be thought of as the route which one specifies to reach a particular destination. There could be multiple logical drives in an os; for example C:, D: etc.

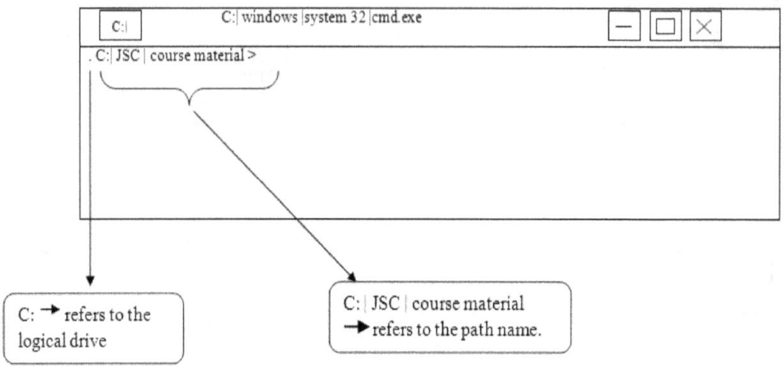

Figure 31 : Example for File Naming Convention in MS-DOS.

In the above example "JSC" and course material are called directories. A directory is a logical grouping of files. In other words a directory is a collection of files with is related to a user or an application. The files are organized on each logical drive within a hierarchical directory structure called a tree. A tree is a hierarchical data structure using a parent-child relationship to organize files. Refer to figure for an explanation on tree structure.

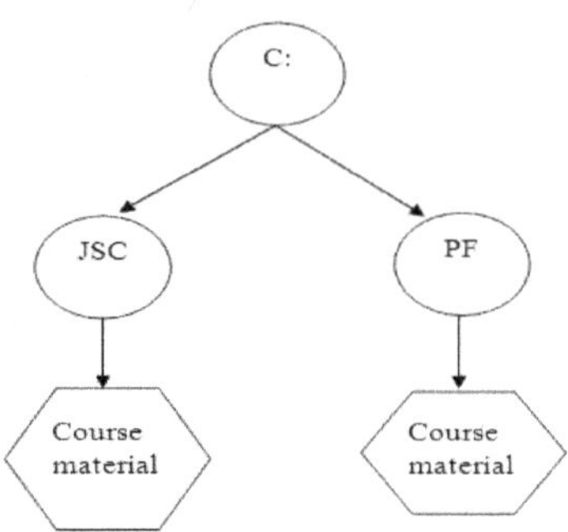

Figure 32: Example for a Tree Data Structure

Top of the directory is known as a root directory which holds numerous files and sub direction. In this example C: is the root directory and it has numerous files and sub-directories. The sub-directories shown are JSC and PF. Each of these sub directories further has sub-directories called course material.

5.2.2. *File Organization in MS-Dos*

This subsection deals with the organization of files in the hard disk in an Ms-Dos. The os allocates disk space based on the demand made by the user programs.

Here for the discussion of the structure of a hard disk. The hard disk is normally made up of multiple disk Platters. Disk platters are similar to a collection of compact disks pilled on top of each other. Normally, the hard disk is made up of three platters. The disk platters is divided into three platters. The disk platters is divided into circular recording units called tracks. The track is in turn subdivided into sectors. A sector can be considered to be the basic data storage unit in a hard disk. A number of sectors make a track and a number of tracks make a disk platter. The set of tracks across platters which have the same radius form a cylinder. So the hierarchy in terms of disk structures is that a number of sectors make up a track and a number of tracks made up a cylinder.

In Ms-Dos file system the disk space is normally allocated in units of a fixed size is called a cluster. A cluster is a collection of sectors. In other words a cluster is a multiple of sector size. Typical size of a cluster are 512, 1024, 2048, bytes. So any new file that is created will have a minimum space assigned to it which is nothing but one cluster. As more data is added to this file, it gets appended to the cluster and based on the further demand additional clusters are allocated for this file.

The clusters can be considered as synonyms with the paging technique which was discussed in memory management since there are multiple files in the system which could be accessed at any given point of time, the cluster allocated for these files may not sit in contiguous in the hard disk. Consider a situation where in a user creates a file, say file A and puts some data into it.

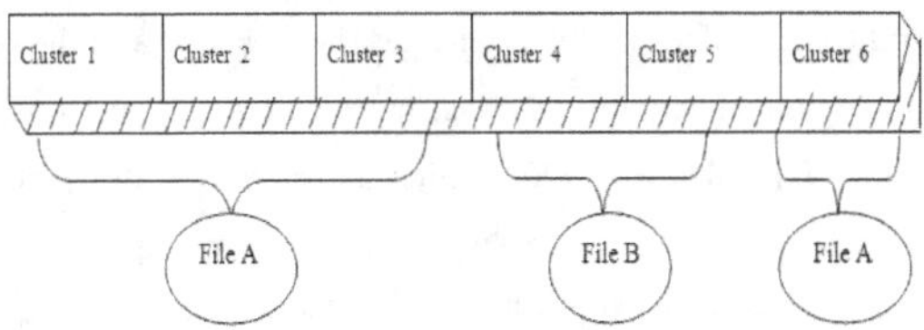

Figure 33: Example for Clustering Based File Structure

Three clusters are allocated to file A. Now this file is closed and another file, say file B is created and some data is put to this file. Two clusters are allocated to file B. Again when file A is opened to append some data a new cluster is not contiguous to the earlier clusters of file A.

5.2.3. *Data access in MS-Dos*

To identify all the clusters of a particular file Ms-Dos uses a mechanism where the next cluster number in the sequence is stored in a table. This table is called the file allocation table (FAT). The FAT is similar to a table of contents that gives information about the clusters allocated to every file in the disk.

The FAT is an array of 16 bit entries. The array index starts from 0. The entries in the array correspond to the cluster numbers of a file except for the first two entries of the FAT.

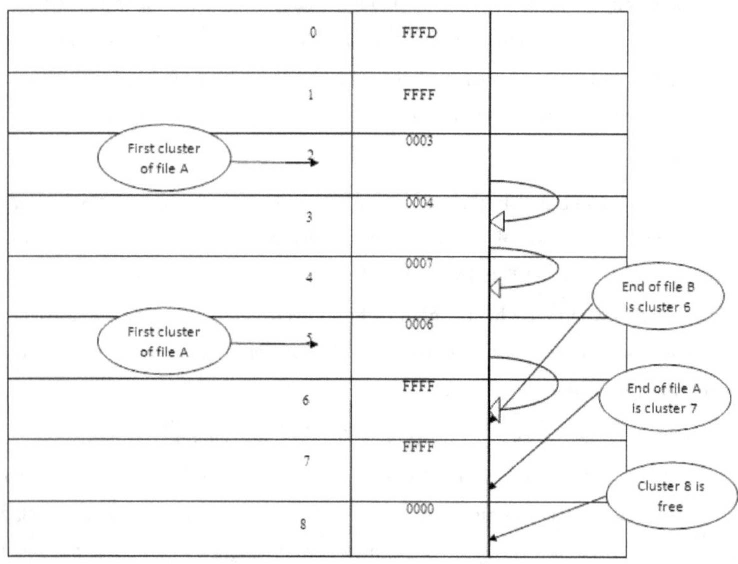

Figure 34 : File Allocation Table(FAT)

The first entry of the FAT which is FFFD. Identifies the disk type and the second entry which is FFFF indicates a value which signifies the last cluster of a file. The first cluster of file A is cluster 2. The FAT entry for index 2 is 0003 which indicates that the next cluster of file A is cluster 3 is 0004 which means cluster 4 is the next cluster. Following cluster 4 is cluster 7 in the sequence and from the FAT entry for index 7, which is FFFF, it is seen that cluster 7 is the last cluster of file A. Similarly the sequence of cluster for file B is cluster 6. Also a value of 0000 in the FAT indicates that a particular cluster is free. In the above diagram (File Allocation table) cluster 8 is free cluster. The FAT mechanism is also known as system of chained pointers as each entry is the FAT points to the next cluster number for a particular file there by forming a chain of pointers.

5.2.4. *Volume Structure of the Disk in Ms-Dos*

The term volume refers to the storage area in the secondary storage. A hard disk can have multiple volumes. The volume structure of a disk defines the way in which disk defines the in which disk is organized.

In Ms-Dos os the volume structure of the disk has the following.

1) *Boot Sector*

The Boot sector contains all information about the disk characteristics. Some of these disk characteristics are the disk manufacturer's name, version and the allocation details like the number of tracks. Per cluster and the number of FATS. (In Ms-Dos os a number of copies of the FAT are Maintained so that it can be used if the main. FATS gets corrupted).

The boot sector also contains an important program called the bootstrap loader. The bootstrap loader is the one of the first program which gets executed when the computer is switched on and the bootstrap loader loads the os from the disk to the main memory.

2) *FAT*

The file allocation table is part of the volume structure of the disk.

3) *Additional FAT(S)*

Duplicate copies of the FAT are stored in the disk which gets updated along with the main FAT. The duplicate copies are used if the main FAT. The duplicate copies used if the main FAT gets computed.

4) *Root Directory*

It is a special kind of directory which has a fixed position in the disk and also the size of the root is fixed. The os programs normally reside in the root directory.

5) *File Space*

Relates to rest of the disk which is used for files and sub-directories.

5.2.5. *MS-Dos Booting Process*

Whenever the computer is switched on, a piece of program called BIOS performs a test to check if the hardware components are functioning properly. This test is called power on self test (POST). After performing the POST the BIOS starts performing the Root booting process by reading through the boot sector in the hard disk loading the bootstrap loader into the Main memory and executing it.

The bootstrap loader now locates the Ms-Dos operating system files in the root directory and loads them into main memory and executes them which in turn makes the operating system function.

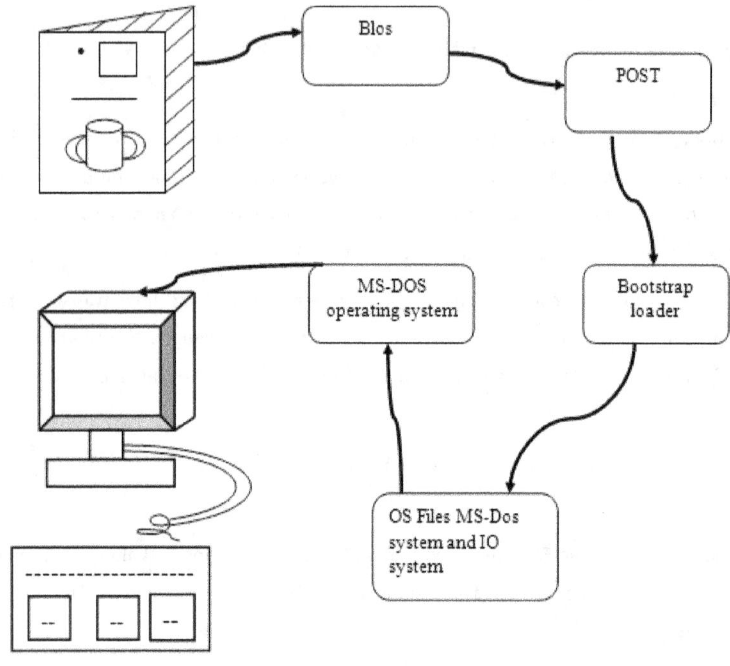

Figure 35: MS–DOS Booting Process

5.2.6.   *Unix File System*

In Unix os the Hard Disk can be divided into Multiple file systems. Recall that a file system is the structure in which files are organized. Analogous to clusters in Ms-Dos, UNIX allocates disk space in terms of blocks. The block size is a multiple of 512 bytes. A file system in UNIX consist of a sequence of logical blocks. There is one compulsory file system in UNIX which is called the Root file system. The remaining file systems are optional and are left to the choice of the Administrator. The file system in UNIX is different to that of Ms-Dos. UNIX file system is hierarchical. At the top of the hierarchy is the root file system which acts as parent to the remaining three file systems, namely file system 2, file system 3 and file system 4.

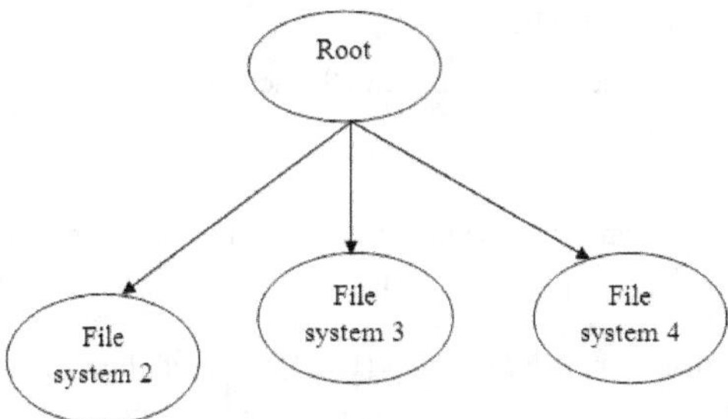

Figure 36: UNIX File System Hierarchy

5.2.7. *File Organization in Unix*

The disk storage in UNIX can be viewed as one which has three components, namely:

1) Directory Entry Table.

2) Inode block.

3) Data blocks.

Directory Entry Table

Every directory in UNIX has a directory entry table which has the following information every file in that directory.

1) *Name of the file.

2) *A pointer to a block which contains.

The detailed information about the file. This block is called node block.

Inode Block

A data structure called inode block is used for describing every file in unix. The node inode block contains information about the file. Every file is UNIX has an inode block associated to it. This is inode block is identified by a unique number inode block is identified by a unique number called the inode number which is associated to every file.

The following are some of the important information which the inode block contain for every file.

1) Type of the file.

2) Location of the file.

3) Size of the file.

4) Last modified time of the file.

5) Last accessed time of the file.

6) A set of pointers to a block which contain the actual data of the file.

Data Blocks

The data blocks are the one which contains the actual data. These data blocks are allocated by UNIX whenever some data is written to a file.

An example of the disk storage for two files (File 1, File 2) is shown in figure.

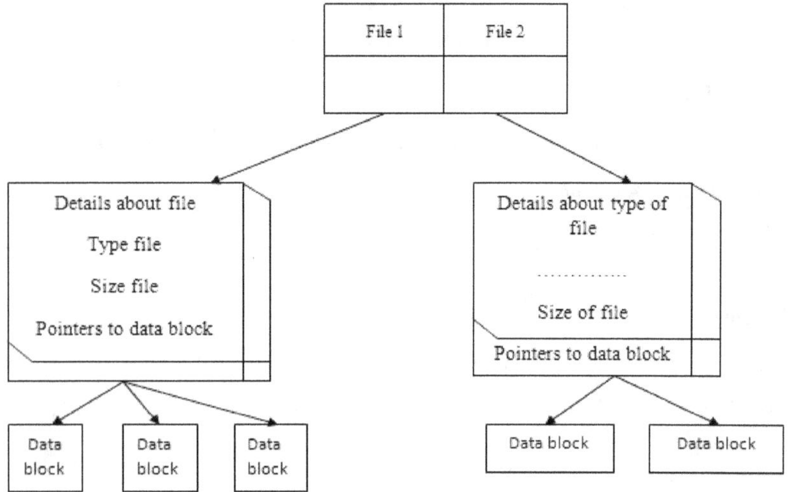

Figure 37: Disk Storage in UNIX

5.2.8. Data Access in UNIX

The mode block for every file has an array of thirteen pointers. The first 10 elements of the array of pointers are called direct pointer. These element point to the address of a data block in the hard disk. Whenever a file is created a data block is allocated to the file store the data and also the first position of the array. The first direct pointer has the address of the first data block that was allocated. As and when the size of a file increases, the os allocated data blocks to it and stores the address of these data block in the renaming direct pointers in the inode block . So, if ten data blocks are allocated to a file then the address os these data blocks will be stored in the ten direct pointers of the inode block of this file. This would mean that the size of the file is 512*10=5120 bytes.

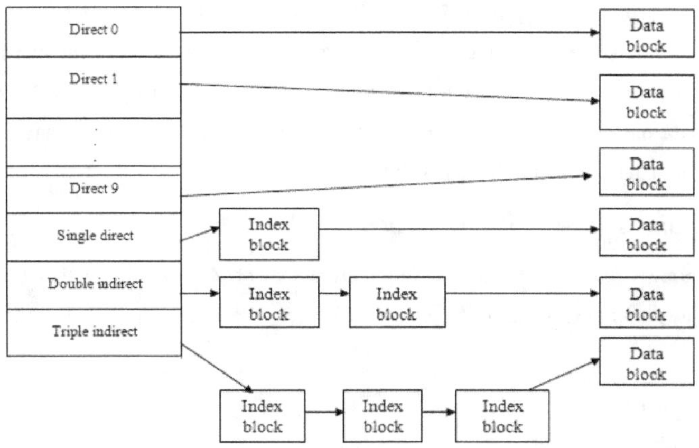

Figure 38 : Inode Pointer Structure

When the size of the file grow beyond 5120 bytes, then the UNIX OS uses the 11th pointer called the single direct pointer, to get the address of the data blocks. This single indirect pointers does not directly point to a data block, instead it points to a block called index block which is 512 bytes of size.

This index block is an array of pointers. Since each pointer occupies 4bytes, the number of such pointers possible for the index block is total size divided by the size of one pointer which 512/4=128. So the index block is divided init an array of 128 pointers. Each of these 128 pointers points to a data blocks of 512 bytes. This is equivalent to 138 data blocks.

Now of the size of the file grows beyond 70656 bytes the UNIX uses the 12th pointer, called the double indirect pointer, to get the address of the data blocks. The double indirect pointer points to an index block of 512 bytes of size. This index block of the 128 pointer which in turn point to the data blocks. In the way maximum size of the file that could be addressed using double indirect pointer would be 128*128*512=8388608 bytes. Hence the total file size that could be addressed using all the ten direct pointers, the single indirect pointer and the double indirect pointer is 70656+8388608=8459264 bytes. This equivalent to 16522 data blocks. If the size of the file grows beyond 8459264 bytes then UNIX the 13th pointer, called triple indirect pointer, which is used to get the address of the data blocks. The triple indirect pointer to get the address of the data blocks. The triple indirect pointer pointes to an index block of 128 pointers each of which points to another index block of 128 pointers. Each of the 128 pointers in the second index block again point to an index block of 128 pointers each of which in turn points to a data block. So the maximum size of the file that could be addressed using the triple indirect. Pointer would be 128*128*128*512=1073741824 bytes. Hence the total file size that could be addressed using all the ten direct pointers, the single indirect pointer; the double indirect pointer is 8459264 + 1073741824 = 1082201088 bytes. This is equivalent to 2113674 data blocks. If the size of the file grows beyond this size the UNIX has a provision include the fourth indirect pointer and so on.

5.2.9. *Volume Structure of the Disk in UNIX*

The volume structure if UNIX is different from that of MS-DOS. Recall that UNIX allows multiple file system to exist in the same hard disk. Every file system in UNIX has the following layout.

1) Boot block
2) Super block
3) Inode block
4) Data block

Boot Block

The boot block contains the boot strap loader which is copied into the main memory when the computer is powered on. The boot strap loader is the first program which gets executed when the computer is switched on, which in turn loads the UNIX OS into the main memory. The boot block is analogous to the boot sector in MS-DOS.

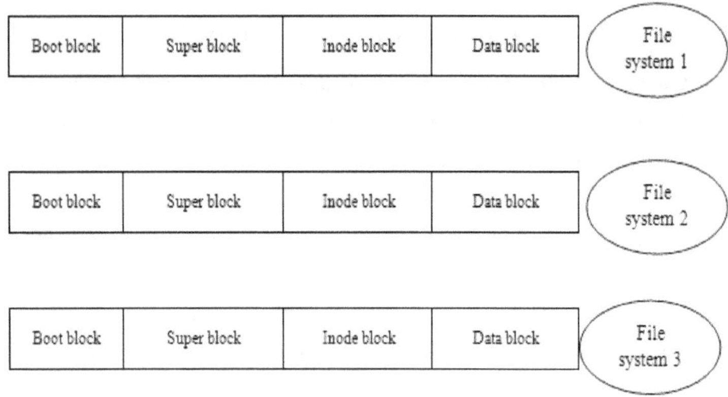

Figure 39 : Volume Structure of UNIX file System

The figure shows three file system as part of a disk in UNIX and all the three have the boot block.

Super Block

The super block has the complete summary of the file system. It describes the states of the file system by maintain the following information.

1) Size of the file system.
2) List of free inode blocks.
3) List of free data blocks.
4) Size of the disk blocks.

Inode Block

The Inode block following the super block and it has a unique record, the inode, for every file in the file system. The inode gives all the information about the file and the disk layout of the file. The inode for every file is identified and accessed by a number called the inode number. Some of the important information.

1) Type of the file.
2) Location of the file.
3) Size of the file .
4) Last modified time of the file.
5) Last accessed time of the file .
6) A set of pointers to a block which contains that actual data of that file. This block is called the data block.

Data Block

The data block contains only data. The information about which data block corresponds to which file is maintained in the inode block.

5.2.10. File Permission

Dos is not a multi-user system. The security in terms of file permission is very limited in nature. On a system with many users sharing the files, is very important to keep a few files private, UNIX is a multi-user ,multitasking, multiprocessing operating system.

In UNIX every user has a username and belongs to one group. For example, username could be Raja belonging to group called. Aug05. There could be others users in the same group. As well there could be many other groups of similar kind.

The files belonging to user Raja could be allowed to be accessed by other group members on even the members of other groups, If the owner (Raja) is willing to do so.

A file could be accessible to read, write or execute. In execute mode the executable files can be executed. The read, write and execute permission could be given to a file in such a way that only the owner can u se them accordingly, or permission could be given to the entire group or members of other groups.

Consider a case where the owner of the file wants to give read, write and execute permission the all members in group and the others as well, then the permission set will be as shown fig 40(a). Similarly the situation where in the owner wants to keep all the access permissions to himself but restrict the group and others to read only is shown in figure 40(b). Figure 40(c) shows a situation where in all kinds of access permission are given to owner but read and write to group and no access permission of any kind is given to the others.

File permission could also be represented in terms of numbers as well. Read is given a value of 4, write is equal to 2 and execute is equal to 1. So in the case of Fig 40(a) where in the users file has Read Write Execute (=4+2+1=7) permission for owner, group and other, we can represent the permission for this file as 777. Similarly the file permission for the case in Fig(b) is 744. Fig(c) is 760.

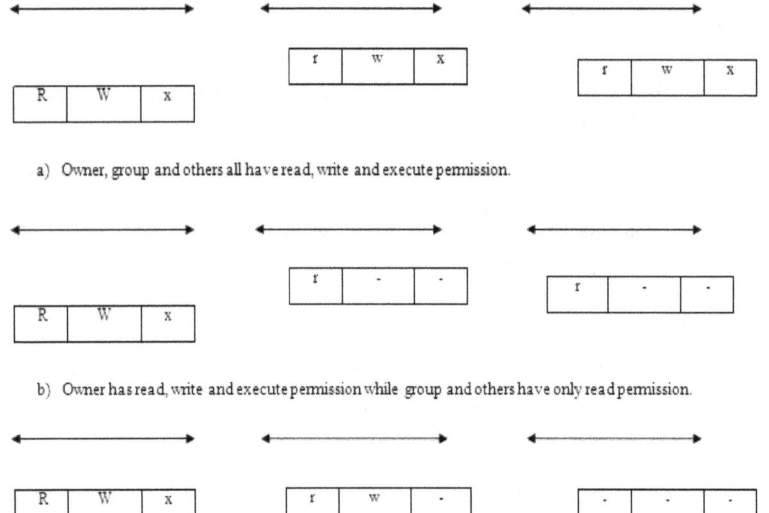

Figure 40: File Access Calculation

5.3.   New Technology File System (NTFS)

NTFS is a file system used by windows NT and its descendants (windows 2000 and windows-xp). This is completely different from FAT file system used in MS-DOS and early version of windows. NTFS has several improvements over the FAT like improved support to store the information of the files and the data structure so as to improve the performance, reliability, security and optimal disk space utilization. Some of the features of the NTFS file system are:

1)   Security and access control.
2)   Size of the files.
3)   Recovery/Reliability.
4)   Long file names.

Security and Access Control

Like in UNIX, this file system implements built in faculty for controlling access to the files and folders in the hard disk. This is a very important feature which was not so inherently built in FAT based file system.

Size of the Files

NTFS supports large file and virtually any numbers of files in the hard disk. Unlike in FAT the performance does not degrade with large volume of data access. In FAT, file system the FAT's would occupy a large amount of disk space themselves. The NTFS uses a different approach to allocate space to the files, thus using disk space efficiently.

Recovery/Reliability

NTFS implements features to recover from problems without any loss of data. In the event of a system crash, the file system design prevents corruption of data.

Long File Names

NTFS allows file names to be of 255 characters in length. In FAT the limitation was 8 characters for filename and 3 for extension names (Example: myfile.doc).

5.3.1.   Overview of the Partition Structure

NTFS divides disk space into clusters as in case of the FAT file system. NTFS supports almost all sizes of cluster from 512 bytes to 64kbytes .But 4kbytes is considered to be the standard one. The NTFS is logically divided into two parts as shown in figure 41:

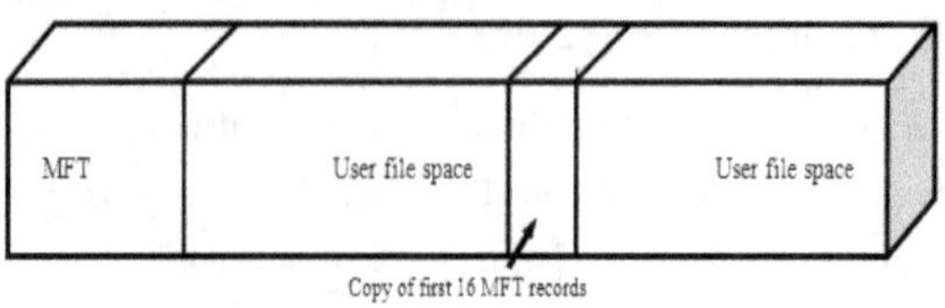

Figure 41: NFTS Partition Structure

The first part in the partition structure is called the Meta File Table or MFT. This holds the information about the other files called the metadata or the metafiles. The other part of this structure is used for the actual user data files. The MFT contains entries that describes all system files, user files and directories. Each MFT entry is given a number. The first sixteen entries in MFT correspond to the system files including #0 which describes the MFT itself. The users files and directories start at #25.

A copy of the first sixteen MFT entries is duplicated exactly at the middle of the user file space. The detailed discussion on the NTFS is beyond the scope of the discussion and is also the proprietary format of Microsoft.

5.3.2. *Limitations of NTFS*

1) The file encryption is not built in NTFS and hence one can boot through the MS-DOS or any other operating system and use low level disk editing utility to view data stored on a NTFS volume. NTFS 5 the enhanced version of NTFS address this issue.
2) For disk volumes of loss than 400MB, the overhead becomes too large.
3) Formatting floppy disks is not possible on NTFS.

5.4. Directory Structure

The file system in a computer can be very costly. In order to manage such entries data, file have to be organized. To keep tracks of files, file system normally has directories or folders, which in many systems, are themselves files. A directory can be viewed as a symbol table that translate file names into their directory entries while considering a particular directory structure, the operations that are to be performed on a directory must be kept in mind. These operations to be considered are:

1) Search for a file.
2) Create a file.
3) Delete a file.
4) List a directory.

5) Rename a file.

6) Traverse the file system.

In order to define the logical structure of a directory, the common structure used are as follows:

1) Single level directory.

2) Two level directory.

3) Tree structure directory.

4) Acyclic – graph directory.

5) General – graph directory.

5.4.1. *Single – Level Directory*

This is the simplest structure. All the files in this structure are contained in the same directory which becomes easy to understand and support. The simplest form of directory system is having one directory containing all the files. Sometimes it is called the root directory, but since it is the only one, the name does not matter much. This structure has limitations like when the number of files increases or when there is more than one user, since all the files are in the same directory. They must have unique names. Suppose if there are two users who make their files by the same name, then the unique name rule is violated and also with the increase in number of files. It is very difficult to recognize the filenames.

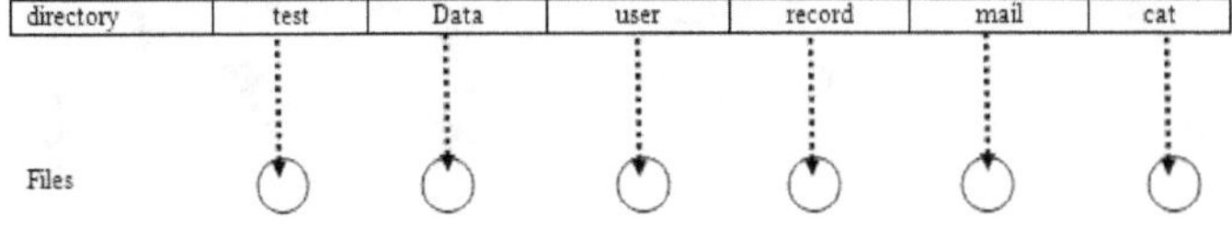

Figure 42: Single Level Directory

5.4.2. *Two Level Directory*

To overcome this disadvantage of a single level directory structure, that is the confusion of file names between different users, create a separate directory for each user. In this structure, each user has their own User File Directory (UFD). Each UFD has similar structure, but lists the files of only a single user. When a user Job starts or a user logs in, the system Master File Directory (MFD) is searched. MFD is indexed by the username or account number and each entry points to the LFD for that user as shown below. When a user refers to a particular file, only his own UFD is searched. So different users may have files with the same name, as long as all the filenames within each UFD are unique. A two level directory structure is shown in Fig:

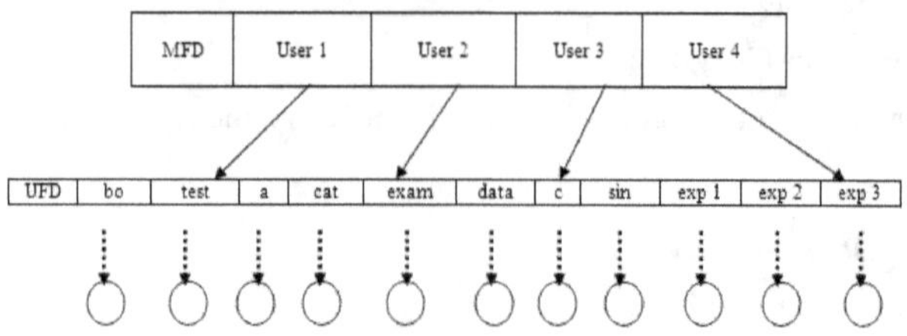

Figure 43 : Two Level Directory

5.4.3. *Tree Structure Directory*

The tree will have a root directory and every file in the system will have a unique path name. It is the path from root through all the sub directories to a specified file.

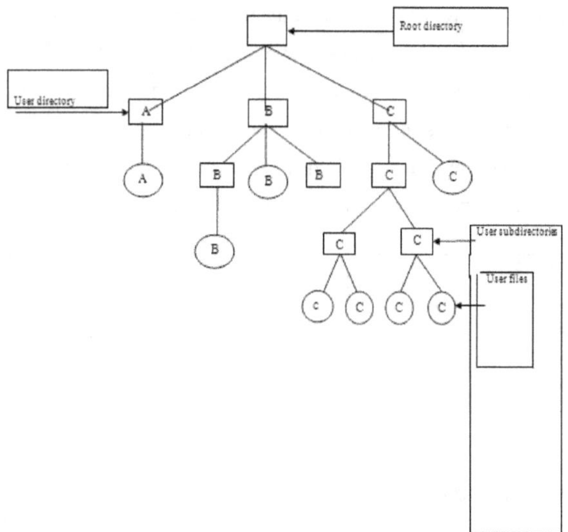

Figure 44: A tree Structure Directory

A directory or sub directory contains a set of files or subdirectories. A directory is another file. All the directories will have the same internal format. One bit in each directory entry defines the entry as either a file (0) or as a subdirectory (1) special system calls will be available in the system to create and delete directories. Normally each user will have a current directory shown the Figure: Tree structured directory.

The path names can be of two types:

1) Absolute
2) Relative

Absolute Path

An absolute path name begins at root and follows a path down to a specified file, giving the directory names the path.

Relative Path

A relative path name defines a path from current directory.

For example ; if the current directory is root / spell / mail, then absolute path is root / spell / mail /exp / obj and relative path may be prt / obj.

In order to delete a directory, in this directory structure, first all the files under that directory must be deleted, that is, it must be made empty. E –MS-DOS.

5.4.4.   *Acyclic Graph Directories*

This directory structure is used in a situation where a common sub directory should be shared. A shared directory or files will exist in the file system in two places at once with a shared file, there will be only one actual file, so any changes made by one user should be visible to another immediately. A tree structure prohibits the files or directory sharing. An cyclic graph structure allows directories to share subdirectories and files as shown in Fig:

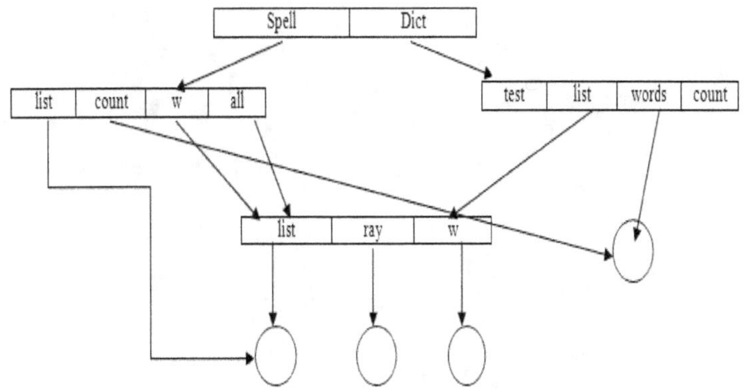

Figure 45 : Cyclic Graph Directories

Shared files and subdirectories can be implemented in different ways. Ex:44 UNIX first create a new directory entry called LINK. A link is a pointer to another file or subdirectory. A link may be implemented as an absolute or relative path name. When any reference to a file is made, the directory is searched. The directory entry is marked as a link and the name of the read file is given. Acyclic graph structure is more flexible than tree structure, but more complex.

CHAPTER-6

DEVICES AND POWER MANAGEMENT

A computer system has a wide range of peripheral devices which are also called Input/output devices. These include keyboard, mouse, monitor, printer etc. These devices are the means by which the computer interacts with the user. The amount of data which these devices can process per unit of time is less compared to the CPU because of their mechanical nature of operation. Hence these I/O devices can become a bottleneck if they are not managed well. The part of the OS which manages these devices, to allocate them a particular user's Job is called the device manager.

6.1. I/O Devices

6.1.1. I/O Channels, Interrupts and Interrupt Handling

Recall, that a database is used to transfer data from one part of the computer to another. In order to overcome the disparity in speed of the operations between the I/O devices and the CPU a separate channel is maintained for the communication between the I/O devices and the computer. This cannel is called the I/O bus system or the I/O channel. The initiation and the completion of an I/O request between the CPU and the I/O channel is done by means of an interrupt. An interrupt is a hardware facility which causes the CPU to suspend its work, save the context of the currently executing process and send appropriate request to I/O devices. The CPU oversees the data transfer and sets appropriate status bit as and when required.

Once the I/O device has completed servicing this request, it sends an .this device. The act of causing the CPU to suspend its work, save the context of the currently executing process and send appropriate requests to the I/O device is called interrupt handling routine. There are different kinds of interrupts like the peripheral interrupt, error interrupt etc which are classified based on their priority. A peripheral interrupt has the highest priority when compared to the other hardware interrupts. After a CPU initiates an I/O request it is necessary for the CPU to get involved in the data transfer during an I/O operation.

6.1.2. Direct Memory Access

Direct memory access (DMA) is a technique which is used to transfer data between the memory and the I/O Devices with the least amount of effort by the CPU. Once the CPU initiates an I/O request, the data transfer between the memory and the I/O device is done directly without the involvement of the CPU. Thus the name of the technique is Direct Memory Access.

Once the data transfer is complete the CPU is notified by means of an interrupt. For DMA a hardware device called DMA controller, which is a special purpose Processor, is used which ensures the completion of the I/O request. All the status bits are set by this DMA controller. A DMA controller has access to the data bus of the computer system and as a result it can transfer the data in and out of the memory.

Whenever a data transfer is required by a program the DMA controller would notify the CPU. The CPU would release its control over the data bus and as a result the DMA controller would access the memory directly without the intervention of the CPU and do the data transfer between the memory and the I/O device which called as the cycle stealing. During this time the CPU cannot access the main memory but it can access its cache memory and it can perform its activity without having to wait for the completion of the I/O request. Most of the peripheral devices like the floppy disk, hard disk, etc. Use the DMA technique.

6.1.3. *Software Interrupts*

Software interrupts are Programmed interrupts. Recall that hardware interrupts are a special kind of device which provides the interrupt facility. Operating Systems provide the facility where in Programs (software) can act as interrupt. In what scenarios would these software interrupts used?

Consider an application Program that is being executed by a user. Whenever the application Program requires a service from the OS like reading data from the disk, a software interrupt also called as trap is generated which will save the current state of the application Program and invoke the file manager of the OS to provide the appropriate service. Once the data is read into memory the software interrupt restores back the current state of the application program so that it could continue from where it was interrupted. The control C-key which is normally used to send some kind of interrupt signal is also a software interrupt.

6.1.4. *Structure of an I/O System*

Whenever an application Program requires any kind of I/O it sends a request to the I/O control System (IOCS). The I/O control system is a set of Programs which is part of the operating systems. The tasks of the I/O control system is to accept I/O request from application programs, do the initial Processing, validation of requests and to route the request to the appropriate device. The application requests are conveyed to the IOCS by means of software interrupts. The IOCS in turn sends these requests to device drivers which are software modules whose task is to convert the application program request, also called the logical request, into commands that the device can understand. In most of the cases each device has a separate device driver. The device driver sends these device specific requests to the device controller through the I/O bus.

Device controllers are hardware devices which control the devices. The device controller gets this request serviced by the hardware and routes the I/O response back to application program through the device driver and I/O control system.

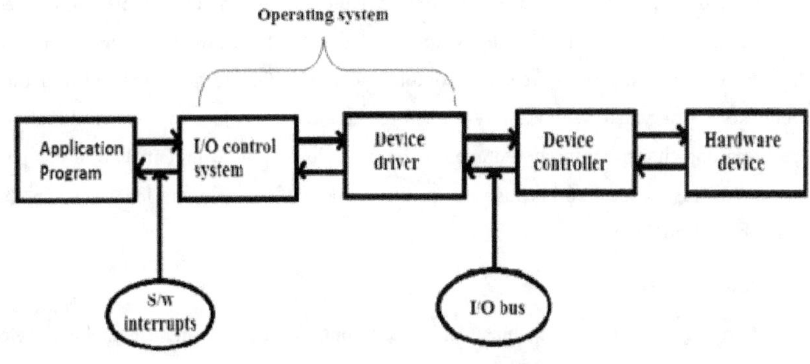

Figure 46: Structure of I/O System

6.1.5. Types of Device Allocation

Consider the following scenario where in a round robin scheduling algorithm is used for allocation of a Printer. Two users A and B want to print files on this printer. Initially user A sends a print request for a 100 page document. Immediately following this, user B sends a Print request for a 20 page document. Since the printer allocation is done using round robin scheduling, the printer would first start the 100 page document and after the elapse of the time slice, say by when 30 pages are printed, the printer would start printing the 20 page document of user B. This way the print out of both the documents would be jumbled up. First 30 pages of user A's document, followed by 20 pages of user B's document and following which the remaining pages of user A's document. This is definitely not desirable. The scheduled algorithm discussed in Process management cannot be applied for device allocation. The following are the two types of device allocation policy that are used.

Dedicated

Some of the devices, like the printer, can be used in a serial fashion one at a time. So if a user A sends a print request for a huge file of 1000 lines then the other print jobs should wait for this print requests to be serviced before they can issue a request. This is one major disadvantage allocation policy as it could lead to a monopoly of one huge print request. To overcome this drawback most operating systems use a technique called simultaneous peripheral operations online (Spooling) where in this all the print jobs are saved in the disk until the print job is completed.

All the saved print Jobs would be printed in the order in which they were saved. Whenever simultaneous operations are made on these peripheral devices, like the printer, the requests are put in a print queue. This queue is stored as file in the hard disk and is called the spool file. Whenever the resource is free, the contents of the spool file are retrieved and the print requests are serviced. Why is there a need to store the print jobs in a file in this disk? The printing does not get interrupted even if the user closes the document that he has given for printing. This is possible because the printing takes place from the local copy in the disk namely the spool file.

Shared Allocation

There are certain devices which can be used concurrently by many users. Such devices are said to be share across users. One example of a device which uses the shared allocation policy is the hard disk. The concurrent access of a device, due to the share allocation policy, can lead to multiple jobs trying to write (or read) data from the same file at a given point of time. The shared allocation policy for the device management in any operating system should bring in a mechanism to protect the data of a file from such concurrent access.

6.2. Power Management

Power management is back in the spotlight for several reasons, and the operating system is playing a role here. Power is a big issue is a battery–powered computers, including notebooks, laptops and web pads, among others. The heart of the problem is that batteries cannot hold enough charge to last very long, a few hours at most. There are two general approaches in reducing energy consumption. The first one is for the operating system to turn off parts of the computer when they are not in use because a device that is off uses little or no energy. The second one is for the application program to use less energy, possibly degrading the quality of the user experience, in order to stretch out–battery time.

6.2.1. Hardware Issues

Batteries come in two general types:

1) Disposable.
2) Rechargeable.

Disposable

Disposable batteries can be used to run handheld devices, but do not have enough energy to power laptop computers with large bright screens.

Rechargeable

A rechargeable battery, in contrast, can store enough energy to power a laptop for a few hours. Nickel cadmium batteries used to dominate here, but they gave way to nickel metal hydride batteries, which last longer and do not pollute the environment quite as badly when they are eventually discarded. Lithium ion batteries are even better, and may be recharged without first being fully drained, but their capacities are also severely limited.

The general approach most computer vendors take to battery conservation is to design the CPU, memory and I/O devices to have multiple states: on, sleeping hibernating, and off. To use the device, it must be on. When the device will is not needed for a short time, it can be put to sleep, which reduces energy consumption when it is not expected to needed for a longer interval it can be made to hibernate, which reduces energy consumption even more.

The trade off here is that getting a device out of hibernation often takes more time and energy than getting it out of sleep state. Finally, when a device is off, it does nothing and consumes no power. Not all devices have all these states, but when they do, it is up to the operating system to manage the state transitions at the right moments.

6.2.2. Operating System Issues

The operating system plays a key role in energy management. It controls all the devices, so it must decide what to shut down and when to shut it down.

If it shuts down a device and that device is needed again quickly, there may be an annoying delay while it is restarted. On the other hand, if it waits too long to shut down a device, energy is wasted for nothing.

The Display

The highest item in everyone's energy budget is the display. To get a bright sharp image, the screen must be backlit and that takes substantial energy. Many operating systems attempt to save energy here by shutting down the display when there has been no activity for some number of minutes. Often the user can decide what the shut down interval is, pushing the trade-off between frequent blanking of the screen and using the battery up quickly back to the user.

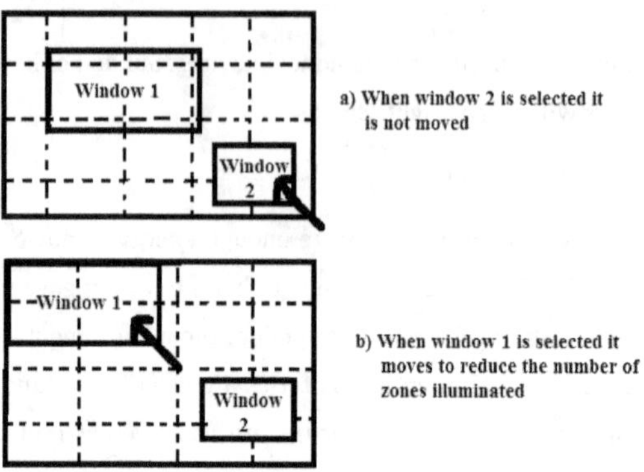

Figure 47: Window/Display

When the user moves the cursor to window 1, the zones for window 2 can be darkened and the zones behind window 1 can be turned on. However, because window 1 straddles 9 zones, more power is needed. If the window manager can sense of what is happening, it can automatically move window 1 to fit into four zones, with a kind of snap–to–zone action as shown in fig 46. To achieve this reduction from 9/16 of full power to 4/16 of full power, the windows manager has to understand power management or be capable of accepting instructions from some other piece of the system that does. Even more sophisticated would be the ability to partially illuminate a window that was not completely full.

The Hard Disk

It takes substantial energy to keep it spinning at high speed, even if there are no accesses. Many computers, especially laptops, spin the disk down after a certain number of minutes of activity. Unfortunately a stopped disk is hibernating rather than sleeping because it takes quite a few seconds to spin it up again, which causes noticeable delays for the user. In addition, restarting the disk consumes considerable extra energy. As a consequence, every disk has a characteristic time, Td that is its break–even point often in the range 5 to 15 sec. Suppose that the next disk access is expected to sometime t in the future. If $t < Td$, it takes less energy to keep the disk spinning rather than spin it down and then spin it up so quickly.

If $t < Td$, the energy saved makes it worth spinning the disk down and up again mush later if a good prediction could be made, the operating system could make good shutdown predictions and save energy. In practice, most systems are conservative and only spin down the disk after a few minutes of inactivity.

Another way to save disk energy is to have a substantial disk cache in RAM. If a needed block is in the cache has an idle disk does not have to be restarted to satisfy the read, similarly, if a write to the disk can be buffered in the cache, a stopped disk does not have to restarted just to handle the write. The disk can remain off until cache fills up or a read miss happens.

The CPU

The CPU can also be managed to save energy. A laptop CPU can be put to sleep in software, reducing power usage to almost zero. The only thing it can do in this state is wake up when an interrupt occurs. Therefore, whenever the CPU goes idle, either waiting for I/O or because there is no work to do, it goes to sleep. On many computers, there is a relationship between CPU voltage, clock cycle, and power usage. The CPU voltage can often be reduced in software which saves energy but also reduces the clock cycle. Since power consumed is proportional to the square of the voltage, cutting the voltage in half makes the CPU about half as fast but as 1/4power.

The Memory

Two possible options exist for saving energy with the memory.

Cache can be flushed and then switched off. It can always be reloaded from main memory with no loss of information the reloaded can be done dynamically and quickly, so turning off the cache is entering a sleep state. Amore drastic option is to write the contents of main memory to the disk, then switch off the main memory itself. When the main memory is cut off, the CPU either has to be shut off as well or has to execute out of ROM. If CPU is cut off, the interrupt that wakes it up has to cause it to jump to code in a ROM so the memory can be reloaded before being used.

Wireless Communication

One of the major issues in power management is Wireless Communication. Here the radio transmitter and receiver required are often first-class power hogs. In particular, if the radio receiver is always on in order to listen for incoming email, the battery may drain fairly quickly. On the other hand, if the radio is switched off after, say 1 minute of being idle, incoming messages may be missed, which is clearly undesirable. One efficient solution to this problem has been proposed by Kravets Krishnan. The heart of their solution exploits the fact that mobile computers communicate with fired based stations that have large memories and disk and no power constraints.

www.ingramcontent.com/pod-product-compliance
Lightning Source LLC
Chambersburg PA
CBHW051131160726
47997CB00018B/1128